Polish—American Folktales

Collected By

Catherine Harris Ainsworth

The Clyde Press
373 Lincoln Parkway
Buffalo, New York

Polish—American Folktales Copyright © 1977 by Catherine Harris Ainsworth. Printed in the United States of America. All rights reserved. No part of this book may be used or reproduced in any manner whatsoever without permission, except in brief quotation in critical articles and reviews. For information, address Catherine Harris Ainsworth, 373 Lincoln Parkway, Buffalo, New York 14216.

Library of Congress Catalog Card Number 77—80771

ISBN: 0-933190-04-2
Second Printing

To All My Students
of the
Niagara Frontier
This Collection of
Polish—American Folktales
Is Affectionately Dedicated

INTRODUCTION

According to The History of Erie County 1870–1970, "the post Civil War boom in Erie County created a large demand for unskilled labor" and the Polish immigrants were meeting that demand, although most "were only passing through Buffalo on their way to the cities further west such as Chicago, Detroit, Toledo, and Milwaukee." [1]

Merton M. Wilner in his history of the Niagara Frontier states that the Poles began to arrive in Buffalo in the late 1860's, "undoubtedly as a consequence of the Polish insurrection against Russia in 1863."[2]

Wilner continues about the Polish experience in Buffalo, which is probably typical of other Polish settlements:

> The number, however, had reached only 135 when the census of 1870 was taken. Their disposition to keep together and to live in the neighborhood of a Roman Catholic church led to the building in 1873 of the Church of St. Stanislaus on Peckham Street, which was placed in charge of Father Jan Pitass. . . . The immigration was checked by the hard times following 1873, but it began to take large proportions in 1878 and 1879. The newcomers were helped by funds from friends already here. . . . Few were penniless when they came, but there was neither work or even sufficient housing for such a sudden influx. The city built barracks to provide shelter during the cold season for some of the poorer immigrants. . . . Within 30 years from the barracks episode, the Polish colony in Buffalo numbered some 80,000 people. They had taxable property assessed above $4,400,000 and non-taxable religious property valued at about $1,500,000. They had well established the character of thrifty, industrious, home-building, family-founding people. By the beginning of the new century the census showed more Poles in Buffalo than in any other American city except Chicago.[3]

The World Almanac and Book of Facts of 1976 recorded 557,478 Polish foreign-born and second generation in the State of New York, according to the Bureau of Census, not including persons of mixed origin, which means one native and one foreign-born parent. New York, along with Michigan, New Jersey, and Illinois, was among the chief meccas for Polish immigrants.[4]

When the collector arrived in Buffalo in 1961, she was told that Buffalo is the second largest Polish city in the world, the first being Warsaw.

The following folktales, legends, anecdotes, family tales and superstitions were taken from my collection of folk material from the Niagara Frontier, or Buffalo and Niagara Falls, area from 1961 to 1977. These are the accounts that were reported to be from the Polish population now settled in the Niagara Frontier section of the United States. Most were written by young people, usually eighteen or nineteen years old, who are of Polish descent by one parent or both. Many of the accounts were told to the younger generation of Poles by older relatives, some of whom were born in Poland.

The accounts are usually brief and well-focused. I firmly believe they were told with faithfulness and sincerity. They were reproduced as they were written with a minimum of editing. Only obvious misspellings and punctuation errors were corrected; syntax was not modified in any way.

The accounts themselves, as well as the discussions preliminary to them, reflect many attitudes and characteristics of the Polish-American group. Many of them are church centered or bespeak a religious tendency. Many have a priest as the protagonist or central character of the account. In them, also, is a definite sense of pride in the Polish heritage. Polish endurance and triumphs in the land of their new settlement are often mentioned. These characteristics and attitudes are similar to those discussed by Thomas and Znaniecki in their detailed Introduction to The Polish Peasant in Europe and America.[5]

The following observations made in 1977 by Robert Olejniczak of Cheektowaga, N.Y., are fuller than the usual comment but are typical:

> Many people in America think that all Polish people have ski in their name. One of the reasons why they think so is because most of the Polish in the United States do have ski at the end of their names. Many of the Polish immigrants that came to the United States changed their last names to names that ended in ski. Because the names in Poland that ended in ski were supposed to be of royal blood, the ski denoted royalty and they wanted to impress people.
>
> During the turn of the century when coming into the United States, it was easy for them to change their names and have it legally be theirs. All they had to do was tell the immigration officer the name they wanted instead of telling him their real name. It was theirs. I was told this by my mother.

Mr. Olejniczak continues with an account about the difficulty the newly-arrived Polish immigrant had in finding work:

> All new immigrants to the United States meet some sort of preju-

dice when coming into the United States. They had to find a way to overcome this in order to make a living. My own grandfather and his brother had to change their last name to get a job. They knew they could not use a Polish last name, so they used a German last name, because the Germans had already been accepted into American society. They both used the last name of Crouse. One of them spelled it with a C, and the other spelled it with a K, Krouse. The funny part about this is they both worked for the railroad. This was told to me by my father.

In 1976, Ellen Cohen of Amherst, New York, reported what her mother had heard from a Polish immigrant, who had settled in Florida and opened a business there:

> In the beginning of the 19th century, there lived this family in Poland with the last name of M_____. The M's wanted to emigrate to the United States, but they couldn't afford to send the whole family over here. The M's only sent their oldest son over here to make a better life style for himself.
>
> When their son migrated here, he was given a job in a restaurant in Florida with long hours. After he made enough money, he opened up his own restaurant called The Famous. . . . After he opened up the restaurant, he then sent for the rest of his family back in Poland. And he hired them to work at his restaurant.

The Contents follow the main outline of Stith Thompson, <u>Motif—Index of Folk Literature</u>.[6] In the discussion that precedes each tale, the motif numbers are from the same source.

FOOTNOTES

1   <u>History of Erie County 1870—1970</u>, ed. Walter S. Dunn, Jr. (Buffalo, 1972), 298.

2   Merton M. Wilner, <u>Niagara Frontier, A Narrative and Documentary History</u> (Chicago, 1931), 499.

3   Ibid.

4   <u>The World Almanac and Book of Facts</u> (New York, 1976), 213.

5   William I. Thomas and Florian Znaniecki, <u>The Polish Peasant in Europe and America</u> (New York, 1958), 87—302.

6   Stith Thompson, <u>Motif—Index of Folk Literature</u> (Bloomington, Ind., 1955—1958).

CONTENTS

A MYTHOLOGICAL ELEMENTS 1
    1. Christmas Eve 2
    2. The Origin of Kgumki 3

B ANIMALS AND BIRDS 5
    1. Christmas at the Barn 6
    2. The Owls 7
    3. The Bear Husband 7
    4. The Cow and the Curse 9

D MAGIC 11
    1. Signs of Death 12
    2. A Message of E.S.P. 12
    3. Blue Dress 13
    4. A Coincidence 14
    5. Evil Eye, Warts, and Headaches 15
    6. The Unknown 16
    7. Seven Brothers 17
    8. The Eel Skin 19
    9. The Baby Goat 19
    10. The Dream 20
    11. Our Lady of Czestochowa 21
        Version 1 21
        Version 2 22
        Version 3 23
        Version 4 24
        Version 5 26
        Version 6 27
    12. Talking Figurines 27
    13. The Mysterious Doctor 29
    14. Godmother Death 29
    15. The Cup of Tea 30

E		THE DEAD	33
	1.	Beware	34
	2.	The Girl's Hand	34
	3.	The Hand	35
	4.	A Bad Boy	36
	5.	The Disobedient Girl	37
	6.	Hung for Murder	38
	7.	The Walking Cane	39
	8.	The Funeral	40
	9.	A Spirit's Return	41
	10.	The Strange Occurrence	42
	11.	Buckets of Tears	43
	12.	A Concerned Priest	44
	13.	The Fence	45
	14.	Back to Life	46
	15.	The Lady Who Swallowed the Egg	47
F		MARVELS	49
	1.	Song of the Trees	50
	2.	Oatmeal	51
	3.	Zmora	52
	4.	Polish Superstitions	53
G		OGRES	55
	1.	A Dance with the Devil	56
	2.	A Witch's Curse	57
	3.	The Pot of Milk	58
	4.	Animal Dung	59
	5.	The Swamp	60
	6.	The Devil	60
	7.	Strange Winds Blow	61
H		TESTS	63
	1.	Boy or Girl	64
J		THE WISE AND THE FOOLISH	65
	1.	The Jolly Tailor	66
	2.	The Lost Ham	67
	3.	The Mean Rich Man	68

K	DECEPTIONS	71
	1. How Krakow Was Named	72
	2. Wawel Tale	73
	3. The Red Tomato	74
	4. A Wise Old Woman	75
M	ORDAINING THE FUTURE	77
	1. The Fallen Picture	78
	2. The Violin	79
N	CHANCE AND FATE	81
	1. The Jack Rabbit	82
	2. The Knife in the Grave	83
P	SOCIETY	85
	1. Christmas Dinner	86
T	SEX	87
	1. Finding A Spouse	88
	2. Polish Marriage Customs	88
	3. A Polish Wedding	89
V	RELIGION	95
	1. The White Lily	96
Z	MISCELLANEOUS GROUPS OF MOTIFS	99
	1. Meet You on Friday	100
	2. An Eternal Jew	101

A   MYTHOLOGICAL ELEMENTS

CHRISTMAS EVE

In December, 1974, Carol A. Petrie, eighteen, of Niagara Falls, New York, wrote the following account of Polish Christmas customs as observed in her family. Her mother, Mrs. Gene Petrie, also contributed to the account. Miss Petrie wrote: "My grandparents had their family together on this special occasion but after they passed away, their oldest daughter, my aunt, continued by having the family together."

The motif A1546.3, origin of Christian worship, might be appropriate in this account.

Before my grandparents died, my mother could remember all the Christmas Eve dinners that she helped her mother make. My grandparents came to America from Poland. They settled in Barker, New York, where they raised five children. During the thirties, things were rough, but not on holidays. The family prepared for a special occasion a feast to commemorate the birth of the God Child.

The supper is called Wilia. When the first star appears in the Eastern skies, the family gathers at the table. Before sitting down to a meal, the family will break a traditional wafer and exchange wishes. I suppose it's still a custom in Europe on a farm to put a thin layer of hay under the white tablecloth in memory of the manger. Also sheaves of grain may be tied with colorful ribbon and placed in the corners of the room to symbolize a good harvest in the next season.

The supper itself differs from other meals because of the number of courses at fixed times, seven, nine, or eleven; and in no case must there be an odd number of people at the table. Some feasters may not live to see another Christmas.

A lighted candle in a window symbolizes the hope that the God Child, in a form of a stranger, may come to share the supper. An extra place is set at the table for the guest.

In Poland, in large houses in the city, trees are placed on the floor or table, but in villages they are hung from the ceiling and are decorated with apples, nuts, candies.

Polish carols are beautiful and sung mostly at Midnight Mass, but lately we eat a Christmas dinner and then go visit some of the relatives we haven't seen in a while.

Here is an example of a Christmas Eve supper: Seven Course: Herring and Pickled Mushrooms
Clear Barszcz (Soup)
Pike with Sauce or Pierogi (Filled yeast dough)
Sauerkraut
Fish
Fruit, Pastries, Nuts, Candies, Coffee

THE ORIGIN OF KGUMKI

The Origin of Kgumki was written in 1977 by Darlyn Sulinski, eighteen, of Ransomville, New York. She stated that the tale began in Poland and was told to her by her grandmother, Alfreda Czarzanowski, of Youngstown, New York. Her grandmother's parents came from Poland to the United States in the early 1800's.

Motif A1426, acquisition of miscellaneous food supplies, might well apply here.

As many of you may know, there is a favorite recipe handed down from the ancestors in Poland. Many people call this recipe "pigs in the <u>blanket</u>", which in the Polish language is pronounced <u>kgumki</u> (goom—ki). This recipe is a tasty mixture of rice, hamburger, and tomato juice rolled up in the leaves of cabbage.

There is an old tale told in Poland on the origin of how this recipe came about. Long ago, a farmer's sow had a litter of piglets. They were all runts and seemed likely to die. So the old farmer cut little strips off of a blanket and wrapped the sickly piglets inside of them.

Meanwhile, his wife was preparing a dish with ground beef, fresh tomato juice, and rice. When she saw what the farmer was doing, an idea came to her mind. She had a head of fresh cabbage and had been pondering on what to do with it. She noticed how the piglets wrapped up in their little strips of blanket looked so snug and comfortable. So, she took little leaves of cabbage and put her hamburger and rice mixture inside and rolled them up. Seeing that she got the idea from her husband, she decided to call her concoction "pigs in the blanket".

B   ANIMALS AND BIRDS

CHRISTMAS AT THE BARN

Christmas at the Barn, so called by the collector, was written in November, 1967, by Gerald Sikora, eighteen, of North Tonawanda, New York. Mr. Sikora said, "I heard the story last week at my great aunt's house. She was born and raised in northern Poland."

The central motif is B251.1.2, animals speak to one another at Christmas. There is also present the motif that deals with premonitions.

Polish legend has it that sometimes animals not only talk on Christmas Eve, but readily converse among themselves with insight into the future. Before this can take place though, certain legendary rituals must be performed.

The evening meal must consist of nine different foodstuffs placed on nine separate plates. Each different plate of food is eaten separately from a small pile of straw. After one plate is finished, the person dining goes on to the next, and so on, until he finished with all nine courses. At the end of the meal all the scraps, are collected together and divided equally among the families livestock. At the stroke of midnight on Christmas Eve, after eating the scraps of the extraordinary meal, legend has it the animals will talk among themselves.

The tale also states that once there was a farmer, who after feeding his livestock one Christmas Eve, listened to the animals from outside the barn. He overheard one animal tell another that the farmer wouldn't care for them next year. At this remark the farmer was puzzled. He never saw another Christmas because he died within a year.

THE OWLS

The Owls was written in 1964 by Barbara Maxson, nineteen, of Hudson Falls, New York. It was told to her by her friend's grandmother, who was originally from Poland. The central motif is B147.2.2.4, owl as bird of ill-omen.

An old Polish folk tale relates the presence of several owls with the death of a family member. This tale is told by the people of Poland and has been carried over to this country by immigrants.

It is believed when several owls gather that a member of the family will die. In an attempt to prevent this death, the person who sees these owls tries to destroy them. He aims expertly with a rifle known to be in perfect condition, and yet he is unable to kill even one of the owls. This has happened several times and the death of a relative always seems to follow.

THE BEAR HUSBAND

The Bear Husband was written in 1976 by Barbara Wawezynek, eighteen, of North Tonawanda, New York. She heard the story, she stated "at our house during Easter" from her mother, Mrs. L. Wawezynek, who was born in North Tonawanda of Polish descent.

The motifs are B601.1, marriage to bear; B601.1.1, bear steals woman and makes her his wife; B633, human and animal offspring from marriage to an animal; and D113.2, transformation: man to bear. Another interesting motif is D721.3, disenchantment by destroying the skin or covering.

One day there were three young girls out in the woods gathering food for their mothers. The girls were having a fine time until a huge bear seized Mary and ran off with her. Mary's friends were so frightened that they threw away everything they had gathered and ran home to tell Mary's mother what had happened. The people of the town set up a search for Mary but they could not find her. So they came to the conclusion that she was eaten by the bear.

The bear, however, took Mary to his den in the mountains and put a huge stone at the entrance so that no one could get in or out except himself. The bear made Mary his wife, and she bore him a little child that was a bear.

During the time that Mary lived with the bear she lost all of her beauty and became black in color with heavy hair covering her whole body.

The bear went out every day to gether food for his family. He even went to the miller to get some flour for Mary to make some bread.

One day the bear went out of the cave to get some wood to make a fire. In his haste to do so he forgot to put the stone back and Mary ran out into the village. When she got there she found her house and knocked on the door. Her mother could not believe it was her. So she took in Mary and cared for her.

Meanwhile, the bear returned to the cave and found Mary gone. The bear got very angry because he believed that the villagers took her away from him, so the bear began to throw rocks at the villagers.

They killed the bear and took his skin off and placed the meat where other starving animals could eat it.

As for Mary, she never lost her black skin or hair that covered her body, but continued to look more like a bear than a girl for the rest of her life.

THE COW AND THE CURSE

The Cow and the Curse was written in 1974 by Susan Tondera, eighteen, of North Tonawanda, New York, who wrote the following:

I heard the story while researching my family tree. I was at my great aunt's house, and my grandmother and aunt were reminiscing about all of the old times as children. It seems that my grandmother remembers the story being told about some of her neighbors during the 1920's in North Tonawanda.

My grandmother, Carrie Tomaszewski, was born February 22, 1909, and she remembered the story about her neighbors and the cow. She was born in Poland, the second of ten children. She had an eighth grade education and became a naturalized citizen in 1922. Presently she is retired and living in the house that her parents owned in the 1920's.

Pertinent motifs are B300, helpful animals; and B301.-6.2, faithful cow refuses to move for grief at master's death.

Many years ago a family had lived in the city and their only possessions were their house, a barn, and one cow that provided them with all of the milk they needed. A lady who lived a couple blocks away saw how productive the cow was and she demanded that the people sell her the cow because she knew the family needed the money to buy medicine for the youngest child who had been sick since birth.

The family had no choice but to sell their prize cow to the woman who had been so selfish. The woman took the cow home and the cow became very sick and would give no milk. The woman was concerned why the cow had stopped giving milk so she went to a spiritualist in hopes that he could find the answers.

He told the woman that the cow would only give milk to people that needed it. He said the cow has a curse on it and will probably die, as would the family that sold it to her, unless she returned the cow and stopped being so selfish.

The woman refused to return the cow and shortly after that she died and the cow wandered back to the original owners. When the cow returned, both the family and the cow regained health.

D MAGIC

SIGNS OF DEATH

The clock episode and the superstitions concerning death were written for the collector in November, 1971, by Karen Smolinski, age eighteen, of Lewiston, New York. She heard the story at home from her mother, Mary Smolinski; both her parents were born of immigrants from around Warsaw.

The legend is an old Polish one, but, she continued, "these things really happened at home".

Related motifs are D1812.5.1.12.1, howling of dog as bad omen; and D1812.5.1.25, falling of shield as evil omen.

In the hall of our home stands a grandfather clock. It chimes every quarter hour and rings at the top of the hour. However, the clock has not rung since the summer and apparently can't be fixed. On November 15, the clock began to chime at 10 p.m. for no logical reason. I was watching television when my mother burst in and said that the clock was ringing because it was my deceased grandfather's birthday. She said that he had come to visit and wanted to be sure no one had forgotten him. The clock chimed at 10, 11, and midnight. It stopped just as suddenly as it had started. It has not rung since then.

My mother went on to tell me that when a person's dog howls for no reason that it is a sign that a member of that family will pass away. Also, at other significant moments, usually an intimate family gathering, a picture or plaque hanging on a wall falls as a sign that the dead members of the family are with us. This occurred at Thanksgiving this year. Everyone sat down to eat. As we said grace, a picture crashed to the floor.

A MESSAGE OF ESP

David Bryk, eighteen, of Niagara Falls, New York, wrote the memorate which he called *A Message of ESP* in November, 1972. He had heard it about three years previously at his home from his father. According to David, his father "has always lived in Niagara Falls. His father had come from Poland so he is Polish himself. At the present time he is not working,"

The central motif is D1812.4, future revealed by presentiment: "knowledge within".

The story I am about to tell is a true story which happened to my father at our house. One night when he was all alone with my dog just thinking to himself as he was sitting in this chair, all was still not even a whisper. Then all of a sudden he had this funny feeling on which he heard the cellar step starting to creak as if someone was coming upstairs. He said it sounded like a floating wave which kept on coming. Even my own dog, who at that time was probably sleeping, picked up her ears and made a funny look on her face as if she had heard it also. This wave-like motion kept on coming until it got into our kitchen, in which my father was just a few feet away and he happened to say something as to who was there and it stopped. He looked. Nobody was there.

Then he had a funny feeling all night. The next day he went to his father's house to see him and found out that he had taken a bad fall that same night downstairs and was in the hospital. We know why he had thought something was wrong that night for he said that wave-like motion was like a message to him of the bad news.

BLUE DRESS

The following memorate, called *Blue Dress* by the collector, was written in 1967 by Wendy Roth, then eighteen, of Lockport, New York. She had heard it at the home of a close friend during the Thanksgiving vacation of 1967.

The central motif is D1812.5.1.2.1, vision as evil omen.

My aunt died in July, 1963, on the fifteenth. Her funeral was the eighteenth. My mother and I were in Washington and my father was at home. The night before the funeral this occurred:

A neighbor who lives next door was outside. Suddenly she saw a lady walking up the street. The lady was of light complexion and wore a blue, high-necked dress. She walked up to the porch of her own home and seemed to be speaking to the house and disappeared. Several weeks later the neighbor was telling my mother about the incident. My mother said her sister was buried in a high-necked dress the very next day.

A COINCIDENCE

A Coincidence was written in 1970 by David Dzikoski, then eighteen, of North Tonawanda, New York. He stated that he heard the story about five years ago at his grandmother's house. His grandmother was Mrs. Josephine Dzikoski, also of North Tonawanda. According to David, "She came from a little town which was located near the eastern border of Poland. But I don't know its name because it was changed when Russia took over Poland."

The story is, strictly speaking, a memorate. The main motif is D1812.5.1.2.1, vision as evil omen.

My grandmother was born in Poland and lived there until she was nine. At the age of nine she moved away from her parents and got a job in Germany. There she worked on a big farm. She was a very small girl and most of the jobs were too strenuous for her so the head of the farm gave her the job of a living scarecrow. She was to chase the birds away from the wheatfield. After the first day, she told the head of the farm that the job was too tiring because she had to run all over the field. She proved to him that she could do the other work and he gave her the job of picking beets. She liked this job and was very good at it, while her friend, named Anne, whom she met at the farm, didn't know how to pick them. So my grandmother would help her out.

One day a letter came to Anne from her sister asking her if she wanted to come to America. She said she would go if Josephine, my grandmother, would. They both did. In the United States, they lived in Utica. My grandmother got married and so did Anne.

Then was the time that the diseases came around and Anne had caught the disease, of which I do not know its name. And one day my grandmother visited Anne with her daughter and her daughter started playing with Anne's hair. My grandmother yelled but Anne said it's all right and it didn't bother her. Then a few days later while my grandmother was sleeping she felt some one pull her hair. No one was around. Then she remembered Anne. A few hours later that night Jospehine's husband came home and told her that Anne had died. She asked when. And at such a coincidence it was when she felt someone pulling her hair.

EVIL EYE, WARTS, AND HEADACHES

The following remedies for the evil eye, warts, and headaches were written in 1967 by Julianne Rajnisz of North Tonawanda, New York. About them she wrote: These superstitious beliefs were told to me by my father, whose parents and my grandparents practiced these many years ago."

The first remedy contains the motif D2071, evil eye, bewitching by means of a glance.

In my father's hometown, Perry, N.Y., many of the older folk believed a person could possess an "evil eye". This was the cursed look a person would give to another and if it was obviously felt by the receiver, e.g., by an upset stomach, then he must try to break the spell before something drastic happened. But, the curse could not always be broken. The way it may be broken, however, was by filling a glass with water and slowly dropping pieces of bread into the glass. It was the action of the bread in the water that determined the victim's fate. It wasn't said what was the exact way of telling the circumstances, but if the bread had sunk quickly, that person was surrounded by evil! Also, the victim was supposed to dip his fingertips into the water after the bread reacted and smear it where he thought would do the best of help. Then, all he could do was wait.

A way to remove warts was practiced by my grandmother on my "poor" father, who later said the warts eventually did disappear from his hands. She baked fresh bread and with some of the dough she put a piece on the wart, wrapping the finger with the rest. Then she gave the remaining dough to the dog. When the dough dried up, it was removed and the warts were soon to disappear, supposedly. My father's father always killed a pigeon and, with a believing heart, slowly dripped several drops of fresh blood onto the warts.

There is a weed called "pig's ears" and this was used to make a tea to soothe a headache or to remove a sty by putting a hot, wet leaf on the eye while you sleep.

THE UNKNOWN

The Unknown was written in 1962 by Marilyn Stevens, fifteen, of Kenmore, New York, who learned it from her aunt. The aunt, in turn, heard it from her mother's mother in Poland.

Motifs appearing are F540, remarkable physical organs; and F555.4, very thick hair. Another motif should be classified under D110——D149, transformation: man to mammal.

This begins in a small run-down apartment in the suburban parts of town. There lived a mother who supported eight children ranging from six months to sixteen years old. They slept crosswise on a double bed while their mother slept in the living room.

One night there was a storm. Rain hit the roof while lightning and thunder roared. The ten year old woke up crying and told her older sister that she felt something furry on her hand, so her sister turned on the lights and searched the room but found nothing. She traded places to see if she would feel it later in the night. Later her youngest sister woke up crying and screaming in the dark. She said she felt something furry near her. So this time they woke up their mother and searched the whole house but still found nothing furry. The older sister said she'd stay up all night and see what it was. Her mother and all the children went back into the bedroom and into the bed.

The next morning they found the girl lying on the kitchen floor covered with fur. After they checked to see what she died from. It was useless. No marks of struggle or blood were found. Just the fur covered her body and death was from shock.

SEVEN BROTHERS

Seven Brothers was written in 1964 by Frank Teibert, age 36, of North Tonawanda, New York. The tale was told to him by his mother-in-law, Mrs. E. Kruzicki, who had heard it approximately 50 years prior from her grandfather, a Polish immigrant.

The applicable motifs are D113.1, transformation: man to wolf; and D572.2, transformation by ring.

Once upon a time, there was a family of seven sons, a mother, and a father who lived at the edge of a forest.

The mother asked the seven sons to go out and pick some berries for supper. The berries were so good that the sons ate most of them, so there were very few berries left to pick when it was time to go home. When the mother saw how few they had picked, she cursed them, calling them wolves. The seven sons immediately turned into wolves and ran into the forest. On arriving home from work that night, the father asked where his sons were. The mother explained what happened and the father took a lantern and went to search in the woods with no avail.

In the meantime, a daughter was born to the parents. This daughter asked why she had no brothers or sisters. The parents explained to her when she was about seven years old that her brothers were cursed. A year later, the father died and the mother became very sick and before she died she gave the daughter her wedding ring and a picture of the father so that she could go into the woods to find them and remove the curse.

When the mother died, the daughter left home and went in search of her brothers. She went to the sun and asked if he could help her get to the other side of the mountain to find her seven brothers. The sun told her he could not take her because he could not reach the other side but that she should ask the wind. The wind took her on his back over the mountain and told her to follow the path. Along the path, in the distance, was a house. However, before she reached the house, a howling wolf approached her. She became frightened and climbed a tree and sat on a limb. Her brothers, still as wolves, were living in that house. They heard the other wolf and came out to see what was happening. The little girl, sitting on the limb, said you must be my brothers because there are seven of you. They looked at one another and she told them that she was their sister and that she came to save them from the curse. She showed them the ring and picture. The older brother recognized the items and they changed back to men. They did not know how they were going to get back home. All of a sudden seven white horses appeared. The eldest brother took the sister with him on the horse and they all rode over the mountain, back to their home. Upon arriving home, the horses disappeared.

THE EEL SKIN

The Eel Skin was written in 1964 by Richard Skwarzynski, nineteen, of Niagara Falls, New York. He heard it from his grandfather, 68 years old, who then also lived in Niagara Falls, but lived in Poland until he was 29. The grandfather stated that the legend started in Europe early in the Eighteenth Century.

It is said that when a person was cut with a knife he had nothing to worry about. He put tne skin of an eel on the wound and it would heal over night.

Many Europeans would go fishing just for the skin of the eel. When an eel was caught they would hang the skin up till it was dried. Later, they would treat the skin with certain oils and bury it over night. The next day they put the treated skin on the wound and the cut would heal overnight.

The Baby Goat

"I hear the story every Easter, wherever our family is on that day", wrote Robert Konecki of *The Baby Goat*, which he told in 1972 while a student at Niagara County Community College. Mr. Konecki of Niagara Falls, New York, said, "My grandmother whose name is Ann Kowalski heard the story from her father. She was born in Warsaw, Poland, and is of course Polish."

The motifs here are D134, transformation: man to goat; and D134.3, transformation: man to kid.

The tale actually has its setting in the countryside. One cold winter night my great grandfather was walking home from a nearby village. He had finished work and was very hungry. Most of the people were in their homes on such a dismal night. As he was walking he remembered seeing a man asleep on the roadside that afternoon. He walked a block out of his way to see if the man was still there. When he came upon this spot he noticed a baby goat lying there. He picked up the goat and put it over his shoulders, thinking that it belonged to a farmer and had wandered away. He planned on taking the goat home for the night. As he walked farther and farther, it seemed that the goat was becoming heavier.

When he reached the crossroads, he stopped and said out loud, "God, you're getting heavy." And a voice from behind said, "I am, huh?"

Then a gust of wind hit his face and when everything had cleared, the goat was gone.

THE DREAM

The Dream was told in 1967 by George Woloszyn, Jr., nineteen, of North Tonawanda, New York. He heard it when he was around nine years old.

The central motif is D1812.3.3, future revealed in dream.

During World War I the family of a Polish officer was reported to have been killed in action. The news shocked everyone, especially his bride-to-be. Every night she dreamt that he was still alive. She always saw him in the same place, in the cellar of an old church. The dream made her so positive he was alive that she began a search for the church. After many months of fruitless effort, she found it. She began digging to the cellar, begging others to help her. They laughed until they heard a voice. There he was alive. It happened that he had been stranded in the cellar when a bomb enclosed him in his tomb. There had been wine and cheese in the cellar on which he lived.

Many people doubt if these stories are true. (See also George Woloszyn, Jr.'s *A Dance With The Devil*). They say that after being handed down so many times they have been changed. Other people just laugh and say that they are absurd. Are they true? Who knows? Maybe they are.

OUR LADY OF CZESTOCHOWA
Version 1

The first version of the popular Polish legend, *Our Lady of Czestochowa*, was written in 1964 by Raymond Roganski, nineteen of Buffalo, New York. He stated that he heard it at home about 1953 from an uncle, Stephan Roganski. He wrote of his uncle: "Born in Poland just outside the city of Warsaw, came to America at the age of 20. Apparently he heard the story from the pastor of the church in which the picture was placed. Returned to Poland at the age of 54, where he died within 4 years."

The motifs present in this church legend are D1624, a bleeding image; D1624.1, the image of Christ bleeds from thrown stone; D1623.1, the image of the Virgin veils and unveils itself, and D1654.8.1, sacred image impossible to remove from the spot. Another motif found in some versions of this legend is D1639.3, images at church turn black as mark of disfavor.

The Polish, being a particularly religious and devout people, have as their patroness the Mother of Christ, Mary. They are especially devoted to her under the title of Our Lady of Czestochowa. Legend has it that this particular image of our Lady was uncovered hundreds of years ago by a young Polish orphan, who was subservient to a landlord in Russia. The lad returned the image to Poland, where it was enshrined in a locale called Czestochowa, from whence comes the title.

Some time later a Swedish invasion of Poland took place. To rouse the sentiments of the Poles, a number of Swedish soldiers removed the image from its shrine and attempted to carry it away. However, the horses were unable to pull the carriage upon which it was to be borne away.

It was as if they were paralyzed. In anger, a Swedish officer drew his sword and slashed the image. The portrait actually bled. To this day all reproductions bear this scar.

Many miracles since then have been attributed to this Madonna. As a demonstration of the devotion of the citizenry of the Polish descent, a chapel dedicated to Our Lady of Czestochowa was placed within the confines of the national cathedral in Washington, D.C. Funds for the chapel were raised by public subscription!

THE BLACK MADONNA
Version 2 of Our Lady of Czestochowa

The second version of *Our Lady of Czestochowa* was written also in 1964, by Clifford H. Hanlon, twenty-four, of Williamsville, New York. He writes of his informant and the background of the legend in the body of the legend which follows.

The same motifs mentioned in Version 1 of this story apply here as well.

The following Polish story was told to me by a friend, Norman Kaleta. It concerns the legends surrounding a painting called The Black Madonna. The painting is real and is now in a church in Czestochowa, a small village in Poland. The subject of the painting is The Madonna holding the child Jesus in her arms. The tone of the face and hands is very dark from which the name Black Madonna is taken. It is believed that the painting was done in the 18th century A.D., but little fact is known and most information about the history of the painting is legend.

The painting was to have been done by St. Luke on the top of a table built by St. Joseph. The painting was found by St. Helena sometime in the 3rd century A.D., who sent it to Constantinople. The Black Madonna stayed there many years until Christians took it to Poland to save it from invading Pagan fighters.

After a time, fierce tribesmen called Tatars invaded Poland. The Tatars tried to find the now famous painting and destroy it, but legend has it that a strange cloud enwrapped the chapel containing the painting hiding it from sight. When the Tatars left so did the cloud.

Acting on the words of an angel who appeared to the people in the chapel, the painting was moved to the village of Czestochowa where it was hung in a shrine.

The painting was kidnapped by Hussites many years later. The story goes that the painting was carried off in a wagon but when the horses reached the edge of the village they refused to go any further. The Hussites threw the painting to the ground and tried to destroy it with a sword but failed. Monks found the painting which was covered with dirt and tried to find water to wash it off. A damp spot on the ground grew into a gushing spring in front of the Monks thus allowing them to clean the painting. No amount of painting or fixing could repair the slash marks carved on the Madonna's face by the invaders.

One other episode of this story concerns an invasion of Poland by Sweden. The Swedes also tried to destroy the Shrine of Our Lady of Czestochowa in an attempt to destroy the moral of the Polish army. The largest Swedish cannon was loaded and fired at the shrine, but before the cannon ball reached its target, it reversed itself and destroyed the gun that fired it.

The painting is honored and adored by the Polish people. The story has served as inspiration for its fighting men for eighteen centuries.

OUR LADY OF CZESTOCHOWA
Version 3 *

This version of *Our Lady of Czestochowa* was written late in 1964 by Tom Stepanian of Niagara Falls, New York, a freshman student at Niagara County Community College. His informant was Mrs. W. Pollsa, also of Niagara Falls, who heard it at a school she attended in Poland.

See Version 1 of this legend in this volume for a discussion of motifs.

---

* Reprinted from *New York Folklore Quarterly*, Volume III, Number 4 (Dec., 1974) pp. 286 – 294, "Polish-American Church Legends" by Catherine Harris Ainsworth

Many years ago when Russia was conquering Poland, there were Russian soldiers in a Catholic Church destroying it. They burned it and all that was left was a large painting.

This painting was of Blessed Mary holding Christ. They tried to move it from the wall, but weren't able to. They gathered more men, but it became heavier. They brought horses to move it but still it became heavier, They still were not able to move it.

Finally one man, tired and mad, raised his sword and cut into the painting. As he did this the painting began to bleed. The faces of Mary and Christ became black. The man died of fright and the rest fled.

This story has been told for many years. The name of this painting is called Our Lady of Czestochowa.

Today, many years later, this belief has not been forgotten. In North Tonawanda, New York, there is a Catholic church called Our Lady of Czestochowa. Here you can see paintings of Christ and the Blessed Mary with their faces this way.

OUR LADY OF CZESTOCHOWA
Version 4

Version 4 of this legend was written in 1973 by Allen J. Zale, twenty-three, of North Tonawanda, New York. Mr. Zale wrote the following about the legend: "This story was told to me by my grandmother, who learned it when she got her religious education. I had to have a translator to understand the story because my grandmother can only speak Polish".

See Version 1 for a discussion of motifs.

Czestochowa is a city in southern Poland. In one of its churches is a wood carving of Mary and the baby Jesus. This carving was supposedly done by Saint Paul. Back in the Thirteenth Century some Polish noblewoman supposedly bought the carving and donated it to her church. According to legend, the ill and crippled were cured in its presence.

In those days of barbarism some thieves supposedly raided the town and ransacked the church where the carving hung. The thieves had a very difficult time trying to remove the carving which really isn't that heavy. In anger, one of the thieves drew his dagger and slashed the Madonna's face. According to the legend, the man died on the spot and the rest of the thieves fled in terror.

Another incident that helped attribute miraculous qualities to the carving occurred in the early Seventeenth Century when Swedish soldiers invaded Poland. When they reached Czestochowa, they ransacked the city and burned the church, which was by now a shrine. The church burned to the ground in a flaming inferno but the wood carving survived. The faces and hands of the Holy Mother and Son were darkened in the flames, but the wood did not burn.

The carving is still to be seen today, complete with gouges in the face which no amount of sanding or touching-up will remove. The highly religious Poles have annual pilgrimages to the city of Czestochowa as part of their Catholic religious tradition which can't be stopped even by threats of punishment by the communist government.

The power of the legend has carried across the Atlantic Ocean with Polish immigrants. Many Polish-Catholic churches in the United States are named after the city where the legend originated. Witness the Our Lady of Czestochowa Church in North Tonawanda.

OUR LADY OF CZESTOCHOWA
Version 5

Version 5 of the legend of Czestochowa was written in 1974 by Marie Gniazdowski, eighteen, of North Tonawanda, New York. She stated that she heard the legend as a child at grade school at Our Lady of Czestochowa in North Tonawanda from a nun, a "teacher with a Polish upbringing".

See Version 1 for motifs.

This story is about a painting of the Madonna and the child Jesus. It was a mysterious painting that couldn't be destroyed, and several attempts were made to do just that.

Poland was in a constant state of war, but its people were God-fearing Christians, and had a painting done of the Madonna and Child in reverence to the Blessed Mother. At one time the Poles fought pagans and these pagans somehow got hold of the painting and because of their hatred for Christians, they tried destroying the picture by burning it. It did not work, but now people sometimes call the painting the Black Madonna because of the dark coloring that resulted from the burning.

The second attempt made to destroy the picture was during a war of which I don't recollect exactly which, but the barbarians at this time tried to cut the painting with a sword. What remains today are two slashes on the face of Mary.

It may be interesting to know that each of the men who tried to destroy the painting died mysteriously soon after. Because of the miraculous preservation of the painting, jewels of every quality now adorn it. They were offerings made to the Lady and Child. It was named The Lady of Czestochowa because it is now located in the village of Czestochowa.

OUR LADY OF CZESTOCHOWA
Version 6

Version 6 of this legend of Czestochowa was written in 1974 by Penny Ziehl, nineteen, of North Tonawanda, New York. She stated that she heard the legend from a friend "on our way to college April 8, 1974". The friend had heard the story from her grandmother, of Polish background.

See Version 1 of this collection for motif discussion.

At the time when Germany attacked Poland the German soldiers took possession of the picture of Our Lady of Czestochowa and took it to Germany. The German King wanted the picture very badly and so the soldiers took it to his palace. Somehow, it cannot be explained, the picture ended up back in Poland again. When the King of Germany discovered this he got very angry and went back to Poland with his soldiers to get possession of it again. The King took the picture and put it on a wagon to transport it back to Germany. It was flying all around. This got the King really angry, as a result, he swung a whip, or something with a sharp edge, which cut the face on the picture. But, this didn't stop the picture from flying about. In his anger the King ordered the soldiers to grab the picture and destroy it in a fire. This the soldiers did but the picture rose out of the fire and consequently, the face in the picture darkened. Where this all occurred a monastery was built which still exists today with the original picture.

TALKING FIGURINES *

An interesting Polish legend, which I have titled, *Talking Figurines*, was written for me by Paul Matikosh, then age eighteen, of North Tonawanda, New York.

---

* Reprinted from *New York Folklore Quarterly*, Volume XXX, Number 4, Dec. 1974, pp. 286—294, "Polish-American Church Legends" by Catherine Harris Ainsworth.

We have in this story the rather familiar motif of the speaking image D1610.21. Motif D1610.21.1. has the image of the Virgin speaking, and another motif, D1639.4., denotes a statue that laughs and reveals a crime.

Mr. Matikosh writes of the legend:

> This legend was told to me by my mother after having been told it by her mother. The story comes from southern Poland and is supposed to have occurred in the late 1800's.
>
> In a small village, an unusually early and severe winter had caused many people to lose their crops. This resulted in a famine that led many people to starvation and death. As was the custom, the people had hung holy figurines in the trees along the paths and streets of the village. These were used to pray to as one walked the paths. It was believed that they would help protect the people of the village. On the edge of town lived an old man, considered by the people as eccentric. It seems that one day he heard strange noises coming from the attic. This is where he had stored his beans which would keep him through the winter. On investigation he surprised a tramp who was eating the beans and taking advantage of the warmth in the attic. The old man, in a rage, bludgeoned the fellow to death.
>
> Several days later, the old man began hearing sounds in the attic. On searching he could find no reasons for it. The noises continued and eventually it became apparent that the attic was haunted. The old man ignored the ghost. After an evening with his friends, during which they had told stories and consumed great quantities of strong ale, the old man journeyed homeward. Confronted by a figurine, he was amazed to hear it talk to him. It told him to confess to the murder. The old man refused. The statue said it would reveal its secret to everyone and it began to shout. The old man, in fear, ran down the path and was confronted by other figurines who also shouted at him about his murder. The old man, now completely terrorized, took off through the forest where no more figurines could threaten him. After a short while, he came upon a small brook which he had never known to exist before. On crossing it, the stream opened up and swallowed him. No one ever saw or heard him again.

The Mysterious Doctor

The Mysterious Doctor was written in 1964 by Mike Kayes, eighteen, of North Olean, New York. The story was told to him when he was very young by his grandmother, who was a Polish immigrant.

D2161——D2161.3 are motifs of magic healing power, under which this tale should be classified. A144, physician of the gods, also applies.

In the mountains between Poland and Czechoslovakia, a strange disease was spreading throughout a small Polish town after a week long meteor shower many years ago. The disease was incurable; no doctors that were called could recognize the disease or had a cure for it. After three days, a mysterious light appeared in the heavens. Promptly a young-looking doctor came to town with a serum that cured the disease. He cured everyone that contracted the disease and disappeared as strangely as he appeared.

The strange light reappeared that night and one week later the doctor's clothing was found on the earth below the spot where the mysterious light was seen. To this day the Poles wonder who the strange doctor was and where did he come from. The most questionable trouble was what was the disease everyone had.

GODMOTHER DEATH

Godmother Death was written in 1977 by Dale Bochenak, twenty-one, of Buffalo, New York. He heard the story at his home four years prior from his father, who was born in Buffalo of Polish descent.

The pertinent motif in this tale is D1724, death as godfather.

The wife of a man had given birth to her thirteenth child and could find no one to be the child's god parent. The man had tried everyone and all refused, so the man said the first person I find I will ask.

While walking down the road he came across a woman dressed in black and asked her if she would sponsor the child and she agreed. The boy grew and turned into a fine doctor.

Now the sponsor who had been watching all these years told the doctor that whoever you see lying with their head at the foot of the table will die. The doctor accepted this and for many years he ran a successful practice.

One day a beautiful woman came to him for treatment and while lying on the table he could see her in the position for death. The doctor, who had grown very fond of the woman, could not let this happen, so he reversed the table and the woman became well.

The sponsor came in and, seeing what had happened, asked the doctor why. He explained and told the sponsor of his love for her. The sponsor then said, "You have tried to cheat me, and I shall take you in her place." Death had won again.

THE CUP OF TEA

The account called *The Cup of Tea* by the collector was written in 1966 by Peter Long, eighteen, of Cheektowaga, New York. He stated that he heard it "about six years ago" from an old farmer, Otto Ranier, who ran a fruit stand.

The motifs are D1402.0.1, magic object burns person up; and D1410, magic object renders person helpless.

In an old rural section of Cheektowaga lived a decrepit Polish man and his wife. In the early 1900's the old man's wife passed away on a dreary Tuesday afternoon. To honor his wife's memory, the old man would have a cup of tea every Tuesday afternoon and set a place for his departed wife. The old man continued this every Tuesday until his death 15 years later.

In the same neighborhood lived a middle-aged retarded man named Bob. He had the mind of a child and was continuously in the company of the small children of the area. One day while Bob and a few small children were playing in the deserted house of the Polish man, they noticed two tea cups and a pot of tea on the kitchen table. As you could guess, it was on a Tuesday afternoon. They came back every day but never saw it again for the rest of the week. The following Tuesday, after the other children had given up the thought of seeing the incident again, Bob and a young girl went to the house. As the girl walked into the kitchen, she was hit in the face with a scalding pot of tea. Upon hearing her screams, dozens of people swarmed to the house and found the mentally-ill Bob huddled in the attic, scared stiff. The young girl never regained consciousness, and died of facial burns.

Bob was naturally accused of committing the murder. The judge said he made the tea the first time to give the children and him a fable to excite their minds. And when the rest of the children stopped believing that the old man was still having tea after his death, Bob became angry and threw the tea at the little girl to prove that the house was still haunted by the old man.

The town sent Bob to an institution where he could do no more harm and he was kept isolated from other patients in order to prevent another rash murder.

A few weeks later a doctor at the hospital found Bob dead in his room. He had killed himself out of sheer loneliness.

The people of the town had been convinced Bob was the murderer until an incident which took place the week after his death. Another wandered into the old deserted house of the Polish man and discovered the hot pot of tea and the cups in the kitchen. As can be expected, it was a Tuesday afternoon, but what wasn't expected was the presence of a third cup on the table. This third cup was that of a child with the name Bob printed on the handle.

E   THE DEAD

BEWARE

Beware was written in 1966 by Louise Placek, eighteen, who was born in Niagara Falls, New York, and lived there at the time. It was told to her the week before she told it by her mother, Mrs. Jeannette Placek, who was born in Poland.

The motif in this tale is E411.0.1, hand of sinner sticks out of grave.

Many years ago there was a teenage boy named Brutus who had no respect for the law or his elders. He was very dissatisfied with life because his parents were poor, and they could not afford to buy him many luxuries. One day Brutus wanted a football, so he went into the local department store and stole one. The police saw him and chased him until he got to his apartment house. The police waited outside while Brutus told his mother what had happened. Brutus not knowing what to do took his father's gun. His mother while trying to stop him, hit him. He turned around and hit her back. He ran out of the house and a policeman shot him.

After he was buried, his hand kept coming up from his grave to be punished. His mother had to go to the grave yard every night and hit it until it went back into its grave. It is said if you hit your mother, the same will happen to you.

THE GIRL'S HAND

Jackie Sroka, seventeen, of Tonawanda, New York, wrote *The Girl's Hand* in February, 1967. Her informant was her mother who told her the tale when she "was little, at home". It is believed to be Polish.

The main motif is E411.0.1, hand of sinner sticks out of grave.

Once there was a little girl whose mother gave her everything she ever wanted. If the little girl didn't get her way she would slap her mother. A few years later the girl died. After the funeral the mother returned to the grave horrified to find that her little girl's hand was sticking up out of the ground. The mother tried to get advice from people she knew, but her efforts were to no avail. That night she had a dream. In the dream she dreamt of taking a branch from a tree and whipping the hand as hard as she could. When the woman woke up she was heartsick at the thought of doing this to her child. But after seeing the hand she knew she must do it. Amazing as it may seem the hand began to recede back into the ground as she whipped it.

THE HAND"

Another version of *The Hand* was written in 1967 by Richard Alan Ciesielski, nineteen, of Cheektowaga, New York. His grandmother, who was born and raised in Buffalo, New York, told him the story approximately three years before he wrote it. The grandmother's parents were born in Poland.

The motif of the story is E411.0.1, hand of sinner sticks out of grave.

There was, as the tale goes, a friend of my grandmother's whose son was constantly rude to his mother and was told by his grandparents that if he wasn't good to his mother, God would punish him. The woman, whose name I prefer not to mention, had found her son drunk one day as he had come home from an all night party. When his mother asked him if he wanted her to help him, he slapped his mother with all the might of his left hand. Two years from the day this incident had occurred the boy was involved in a car accident and died on the way to the hospital, crying for his mother until he had expired. When the woman's son was buried, the mother prayed for him and knew that God had taken vengeance, but the wrath of the Almighty wasn't over. Therefore, every Mother's Day the hand of the boy would ascend from the grave, the hand he had hit his mother with, and his mother together with a priest would beat the hand of her son back into its grave with a club of wood. As the story goes, this incident would take place every Mother's Day until his mother had passed away. This story is said to be real but it might be questionable. The cemetery involved is said to be the Old Saint Stanislaus Cemetery on Pine Ridge Road in Cheektowaga, New York.

A BAD BOY

A Bad Boy was written in 1964 by Edward F. Cholewka, seventeen, of Sloan, New York, who heard it when he was in the second grade at St. Andrew's School in Sloan, a school "basically Polish in background".

The dominant motif is E446.3.1, ghost laid by beating body to pieces.

Around and about the late eighteenth century, the place is not really important for it could have been a small community in England or a town in the countryside of New England, a series of strange events took place around the grave of the newly buried body of a seven-year-old boy. Shortly after he was buried, the earth around the wooden box which held him was violently disturbed and the boy himself left lying, half covered by dirt, half exposed to the elements, in broad view of the church in which he was buried. The following day, Sunday, as the laymen and the clergy were readying themselves for church services, the body was discovered. The deeply religious populace was horrified at the way in which the upheaval of the grave's dirt was speculated to have occurred. It almost seemed that the corpse had dug itself out of its own grave. But, another view took the belief of the general majority of the good town's people and that was the belief that graverobbers had dug up the fresh corpse in the hopes that they could exchange it to a biologist for an amount of money. Biologists, claiming to be just scientifically curious, and the infamous grave robbers, who aided them, were looked upon as friends in this particular area of the world. It was further speculated that since the body was so small, the fiends didn't think it worth stealing. However, shortly after the body was reburied, the same thing occurred. For the third, and hopefully the last, time, the body was buried. It happened once again. This time the strongly religious community felt that the devil was behind this grotesque deed. They summoned a church leader to the scene who, in turn, summoned the boy's parents. They revealed to the clergyman that the boy, in life, had never been punished, though he was responsible for many of the deeds of destruction done in town. It would seem as if the earth vomited out such an evil being as he was. The chief clergyman's decision was that the parents beat the body. They whipped the corpse unmercifully until his bones showed. All left the graveyard and, in the morning, the corpse was in his casket, the ground over the grave was smoothed over and a thick green grass was growing there.

THE DISOBEDIENT GIRL

The Disobedient Girl was written in 1974 by Fred Gadawski, eighteen, of Niagara Falls, New York. He heard it in 1966 when he was in the fifth grade at Holy Trinity School from his teacher, Sister Mary Juliette.

The motifs are E446.3.1, ghost laid by beating body to pieces; and E411.0.1, hand of sinner sticks out of grave.

There once was a girl who never obeyed or respected her parents. One day she was told by her mother to stay home. In rebuttal to the mother's command, she proceeded to storm out of the house. Her mother was angry and chased after her and caught her. The girl turned to her mother and raised her arm and hit her. The mother let go and the girl ran out.

That night the girl was found dead in a field. When the girl was buried in two days, the hand which she struck her mother with stuck out above the grave. A priest told the mother the hand was above the grave because the girl was repenting her disobedience sin and the mother would have to beat the hand with a stick till it goes under again. And she'll have to beat it under every time it comes up.

HUNG FOR MURDER

The following story was written in 1964 by Gerald Wienckowski, seventeen, of Depew, New York.

The motifs that apply to this account are E446.3.1, ghost laid by beating body to pieces; and E411.0.1, hand of sinner sticks out of grave.

Mr. Wienckowski wrote the following information about his story; "The story which I am about to tell was told to me by my grandmother when I was first learning right from wrong. This same story was told to my grandmother by her mother and was passed on through the family line. Whenever small children form a habit of hitting their parents when the parents scold or spank them, this story is to be told so it will break them of the habit. This story begins something like this":

There was a small boy who was as normal as any other boy except he had a bad habit of slapping his parents' hand whenever they would reach out to spank him. This habit would just grow worse whenever the parents would attempt to break it by hitting him more or some other similar way. As the boy grew up, this bad habit grew with him. At one time in his life, he and his father had a big argument and his father slapped him and the boy swung and hit his father and killed him. The boy was then put on trial and hung for murder.

Well, I guess this story might help some poor child off the wrong path in life; it helped me.

THE WALKING CANE

The Walking Cane, a title given by the collector, was written in 1968 by Joseph Tarnowiecki, eighteen, of Niagara Falls, New York. He wrote: "I heard this story at home about eight years ago and had the story retold to me just a few days ago to refresh my memory. My informant was my sister, who originally came from Poland. She acquired the story from my grandmother who told it to her when she was a child and lived in Poland.

Related motifs are E530, ghosts of objects; E539, other ghostly objects; E539.4, ghostly chair; and E402.3, sound made by ghostly object.

There once was an old man who lived by himself on the far outskirts of a town in the country. He made his living by making small toys and other gifts for children, which he sold in the town square. Each day the old man would walk to town in the morning and leave at dusk, taking whatever money he had made. Because he was such an old man, his legs had become weak and he used a cane to help him walk the great distance from the country to the center of town. Many of the town's children liked the old man since he often gave them the gifts he made, for their companionship. There was one group of older boys, although, who did not like the old man and would often tease him about being crippled and having to use the cane to help him walk. It was to these boys that the old man never gave gifts, for he felt that they would not appreciate them anyway.

One night when the old man was walking home, the group of older boys approached him. They began teasing him calling him a helpless cripple and reprimanded him for not giving them any of his gifts. Then one of the boys pushed the old man, while the rest of them took his cane and broke it. When the boys had left, the old man managed to get up and sorrowfully make his way home. There, he was found dead four or five days later by some townspeople who began to get worried about him when he no longer came to town. The people then laid him away to rest peacefully, near his meager home.

The next day after the burial, the group of boys who had caused the man's death all came to the town's square and arranged to meet to have some fun that night at their usual meeting place. That night when the boys had assembled together, one of them noticed something strange coming toward them, that was making a strange sound. It sounded like wood mixing with the sound of the stone road and was coming from the center of town. Then all at once, as it seemed, they all noticed that it was a cane which had been broken, striking the ground but with nothing holding it. Upon seeing this, the boys thought that the old man's ghost had come to get them and they all ran off trying to make their way to their homes.

Over the next few weeks the townspeople had noticed a remarkable change in the attitude of the boys toward other people since they were always trying to help instead of poke fun at others. But what was even more strange, was that somehow the old man's cane had found its way to the old man's grave after being gone for such a long time and no-one really knew how it had gotten there.

After that the townspeople often said that if one listened very closely, he could hear the sound of a cane striking the pavement at the turn of dusk, slowly making its way out of town.

THE FUNERAL

The Funeral was written in 1964 by James Mamon, eighteen, of Niagara Falls, New York, who heard the story from his grandmother about two years prior. The grandmother had heard the story when she was a little girl in Poland.

The burying of live persons, believed dead, should be considered with the E motifs concerning the dead. E127, for instance, is the resuscitation from the dead by friends.

Years ago, around the turn of the century the ritual of a funeral was not as momentous an occasion as it is today. In fact, the corpse was not embalmed unless requested by the immediate family. This brings to mind a tale of horror that occurred in that era.

It was a normal day for a funeral, dark and drizzly. A small group of people gathered at the cemetery to pay their last respects before the coffin was to be lowered into the cold earth. As the crowd began to depreciate, the caretakers were patiently waiting to add on the finishing touches. When everyone had left, one of the three caretakers became curious as to what the corpse would look like after a couple of days of lifelessness. All agreeing, they decided to open the coffin. With his shovel, one of the men began to pry open the top. The rain came down heavier, and the two other men thought of abandoning the idea. However, the top slipped open just as they were ready to quit.

The lightning crashed, and the three men stood motionless at the sight they beheld. Before them, the corpse of a woman lay silent, but what was it that made these men stare in shock and amazement? The body was not lying on its back as normal, but face down. From what the men could distinguish, she had rolled over in an attempt to free herself from this wooden bondage in which she was prematurely placed.

A SPIRIT'S RETURN

The following belief tale, entitled *A Spirit's Return* by the collector, was written in 1967 by Barbara Szlachtun, seventeen at the time, of Tonawanda, New York. She stated that she heard this tale when she was a little girl and again in February, 1967, at her home. "My mother and father told me this tale, which also happened to them," she wrote.

The main motif is E320, dead relative's friendly return.

It had been part of Polish tradition to believe that after someone had died, his spirit came back and visited all of his close friends to tell them that he had died. My uncle didn't believe this. He said that after a person died, he was dead for good. There was no such things as spirits. Spirits were all just part of a superstition. Soon my uncle got cancer, and he went to the hospital. One night his spirit came to our house. My parents were in bed when they heard his footsteps climb up the stairs. Then the bolted door opened. His spirit came into the house, entered their bedroom, touched my father, and then left after he had closed and rebolted the door to the outside. The next morning, when the telephone rang, my parents told my relatives that they had already known that my uncle had died. He had died only a few minutes before he had paid my parents his visit. My relatives were shocked to hear that, and ever since that day, no one in our family has doubted that spirits exist.

I know some other tales that my father has told me. However, I do not know the reasons behind most of them. It is considered bad luck if you put your hat on the bed and leave it there for a period of time. Also, if you shake hands in a funeral home, you should be careful not to cross them. The Polish people believe that if you do cross them, one of the people that crosses them will soon die. In the past generation of our family, there have been instances where this has been true.

THE STRANGE OCCURRENCE

The Strange Occurrence was written in 1974 by Rose Garaczkowski of North Tonawanda, New York. Her informant was a member of her family, Stanley Owcarz, who was born in 1937 in the small coal-mining town of Gallitzin, Pennsylvania. "His parents immigrated to the United States from Poland and settled in Pennsylvania. His father worked there in the coal mines. He had seven brothers and three sisters. He is now a married man with two teenage daughters and a twelve year old son living in Buffalo, N.Y." This is the brief history of the informant in the words of Mrs. Garaczkowski.

The central motif is E300, friendly return from the dead.

About 30 or 40 years ago in Gallitzin, Pennsylvania, my brother-in-law's brother, Frank, went to a square dance with his friends. It wasn't too late when the dance ended so they went to a friend's house to have a few drinks and play cards.

About 2:00 a.m. he started home. After he had walked for a while he thought he heard footsteps but when he turned around nobody was there. So he started walking faster but the footsteps came closer and closer. He was very frightened; he heard someone call him and turned to look. He could see nobody but the voice intermittently talked to him and he could now recognize that voice as Mr. Beets, a family friend and neighbor. When he was about 30 yards away from his house the voice said, "Goodnight, Frank, and thank you for talking with me."

When Frank went in the house he was babbling to himself about his unusual experience. His mother wanted to know what was wrong when she heard and saw the state he was in. It took him about fifteen minutes to calm down enough to relate the tale. His mother stared blankly at him and told him Mr. Beets had died four hours earlier.

BUCKETS OF TEARS

Buckets of Tears was written in 1970 by Christine Skowron, eighteen, of Niagara Falls, New York, who heard the story when she was about five or six at her grandmother's house. Her grandmother, Caroline Tyran, came to America from Oswiemcim, Poland, when she was about fifteen.

The motifs present in this account are E324, dead child's friendly return to parents, frequently to stop weeping; and F1051, prodigious weeping, usually by saint.

The story I heard was about a middle aged woman whose three young children had died. The woman lived in a very small village and the grave yard where her children were buried was about a half mile outside the village. Every morning the woman would walk to the cemetery and cry for hours over the graves. The people in the village tried to get her interested in other things, but she wouldn't listen to them. One morning she came running back from the cemetery very frightened. She told the priest that as she approached the cemetery she saw three very tall men with buckets of water hanging from their shoulders. The water was over flowing from the buckets. The men were weeping and the closer she got to them the bigger the men appeared. She became very frightened and ran away. After listening to her story the priest sait it was a sign. It was a way the three children had of telling the mother to stop grieving. Their mother's grief was wasted, like the water spilling out of the buckets. The priest told the woman not to go to the cemetery again, but to start a new life for herself.

A CONCERNED PRIEST

A Concerned Priest was written in 1972 by Gail Dojka, nineteen, of Niagara Falls, New York. About this legend she wrote: "I heard this story from my grandmother on Easter. This story was told to her by her father who supposedly it happened to. My grandmother was born in Poland but lived in Niagara Falls the majority of her life. Her name is Genny Keller.

One motif is E443.2.4.1, ghost laid by group of ministers, by prayer and services, usually with "bell, book, and candle" or some modification of the procedure.

Before I begin it is best to know that my great grandfather played the organ for a church and kept some of their records. Just prior to the incident the pastor of his church died.

One night my great grandfather sat down in his living room and began to read. Before he could even get started the candle blew out. He decided it was drafty in the room and lit it again. The candle blew out for the second time. He then went to bed figuring there was no use in trying to read that night.

The next night he attempted to read again and again the candle blew out. With no further attempts he went to his bedroom and to his amazement he found the bed had been moved to the other side of the room. He assumed that his housekeeper may have moved it but he couldn't figure out why. He changed and went to bed. As soon as he got in the bed it began to move back and forth but when he jumped off it stopped.

Since his pastor had just died and he believed this incident to be some kind of spiritual phenomenon he connected the two together. He looked through some of the papers he had concerning church affairs and found a small piece of paper with a list of names of people who had died a few months before. These people were supposed to have masses said for them but they had somehow been overlooked.

The next morning he went to various pastors and gave them each a name from the list in order to have a mass said for them.

After the masses were said he no longer had any trouble with beds moving or lights blowing out. My great grandfather deducted from this experience that the pastor had forgotten to give these masses and couldn't rest until these people received the help they needed to get to heaven from these masses.

THE FENCE

The Fence, so called by the collector, was written in 1967 by Lori Sarama, seventeen, of Amherst, New York. She heard the tale when she was about ten or eleven years old and living in Buffalo from her great-grandmother, who grew up in Poland.

The motifs are E337, ghost reenacts scene from own lifetime; and F1041.7, hair turns gray from terror.

Back in Poland there was a party for young people. Some of the couples decided to go for a horse and buggy ride. When they returned, their hair had turned white. They told their story as follows:

While they were riding down a dark road they saw a man standing near one of the stone fences used to divide their property. He was holding one of the large stones and swaying it back and forth. He kept saying, "Where shall I put it, where shall I put it?" When one of the people told him to put it down, he said thank you and put it down. All of a sudden, the man turned to a skeleton and then to dust. It was said that the man had moved the fence a few feet to increase the size of his property and after he had died, had to come back as a punishment.

BACK TO LIFE

Back to Life was written in 1964 by John Kaspezak, eighteen, of Niagara Falls, New York. He heard this custom from his grandmother, who came to America from Poland.

The motif is E162.1, resuscitation even possible after three days.

It was the custom in Poland that when a person died certain men in the neighborhood would watch the body all thru the night. These men sat, played cards and drank throughout the night. While they played cards a certain man saw the dead person's head or arm rise he thought he was seeing things, but then many people who were in a coma were buried alive, thinking they were dead. This led doctors to thoroughly check the body before pronouncing them dead.

THE LADY WHO SWALLOWED THE EGG *

The Lady Who Swallowed The Egg was written in 1965 by Mary Ann Jasek, eighteen, of Niagara Falls, New York. She stated that she heard the tale "last year" at her aunt's house.

This tale has as its central motif that of resuscitation. Although these motifs are numerous, E0 to E199, the exact one of resuscitation by removal of an egg is not among them. E21, resuscitation by withdrawal of wounding instrument, is found, according to Thompson, in the lore of Italy, of India, of the North American Indians, and of the Eskimos.

Polish peasants, like all peasants, get enjoyment from telling and listening to stories which are generations old. Here is one my great-aunt brought with her and passed on.

The day before Easter, the Polish people take a basket of food to church to be blessed.

There was a peasant family who lived in the country and had quite a distance to drive to the church. The father and his children were dressed and ready, but they were still waiting for his wife, who was still dressing. He kept yelling up to her room to hurry. She was dressing as fast as she could. She put on her pearls and her hat, but she was hungry. She took a hard-boiled egg from the basket. Her husband kept yelling louder and louder, so instead of breaking open the egg, she swallowed it whole. The egg caught in her throat and she fell to the floor.

Her husband kept yelling, but after hearing no response, he went up to investigate and found his wife dead. In those days, there were no embalming methods, and the dead were buried quickly in a simple pine box. The husband put his

---

* Reprinted from *New York Folklore Quarterly*, Volume III, Number 4 (Dec., 1974) pp. 286-294, "Polish-American Church Legends" by Catherine Harris Ainsworth.

dead wife in the wagon, took her to church, and had her buried.

That evening, he remembered his wife was wearing her expensive pearls. He decided to dig up her grave and take them back. He went to the graveyard, dug up the ground, and opened the casket. He put his knee on her chest and lifted her head to unlock the clasp. Just then his wife woke up. She had swallowed the egg which had been caught in her throat. Her husband was so frightened, his hair turned grey, and he fell down dead.

The lady got up, put him into the coffin and covered up the grave. Then she went home to celebrate Easter with her children.

F   MARVELS

THE SONG OF THE TREES

The Song of the Trees was written in 1964 by George L. Kraus, age thirty, of Buffalo, New York. His informant was Dennis Gorski, also of Buffalo, who heard it when a child from his mother. His mother was told the story by her mother. It goes back to Warsaw, Poland.

The central motif is F979.3, leaves of tree make melody for saints. The aeolian harp or wind music in the trees is a favorite image among the writers of the Romantic Age of English literature.

Somewhere in the rural area surrounding Warsaw, Poland, there is a legend among the farmers. It seems that country folks meet in a certain valley and have a picnic early every Sunday. They all arrive by horse and wagon dressed in their folk clothing. Grandmothers, grandfathers, mothers, fathers, and grandchildren are there. All day long they eat, laugh, and are merry. Many tall and huge trees can be found in and around this valley. Each Sunday at about seven o'clock, the wind blows through the trees in a strange way. The howling of the wind blowing through the trees produces a melody like that of musical instruments playing in a symphony orchestra. The people are familiar with this melody because it is always the same. Everyone joins in singing a song to the melody which is called "The Song of the Trees".

OATMEAL

The following tale, called *Oatmeal* by the collector, was written in 1964 by Richard Stepniewski, nineteen, of Buffalo, New York. He reported that he first heard the story in Germany when he was very young. Then he asked his mother to retell it. She had heard it from a man in one of the displaced person's camps in the late 1940's.

One motif here would probably come under F950, marvelous cures.

Shortly after the war, there were many displaced persons in Germany. My parents were in this category. They could not return to their native Poland and it was not until 1951 that they were allowed to come to the United States. The six years following the war were spent in about a dozen displaced person's camps.

In these camps, the favortie pastime was to go to your friends and spend the evening telling each other various tales and stories. Young though I was, I used to enjoy the crazy and unusual tales that the adults told to each other. The following story was first told to my parents by the camp's best story teller.

During the Eighteenth Century, the medical profession in Poland (and in Europe) was not a science as it is today. If you became sick, you consulted your neighbors and after receiving many opinions and cures, you decided which was best and used it.

Well, it happened that a man became quite sick. He developed a rash and many sores came out on his skin. The family was told that if they cooked some oatmeal and covered his skin with it, the man would get well. This was done but the patient still died. To prepare the man for burial, the family took the oatmeal——and also some of the diseased sores off his body and placed it in a large pot near the stove.

While the whole family went to the church for the burial, two vagabonds came to their home. They were very hungry so they began looking through the house for food. They could not find any food but they did find the oatmeal and they ate it. Just as they were finishing the oatmeal, the family arrived from church. The vagabonds thanked them for the food they ate but the father did not know what they were talking about, since he knew that his home did not have any food.

The misunderstanding was cleared up when the vagabonds mentioned the oatmeal. They were then told the purpose of the oatmeal. Ever since then, there were two vagabonds in Poland that always asked the origin of their meal.

ZMORA

Zmora was written in 1977 by Sharon Catalfo, twenty, of Niagara Falls, New York. She heard the story from her grandmother, Rose Kruzel, living in Buffalo, who heard it from her grandmother, "and it happened in the 'old country', Poland".

The obvious motif is F471.2.1, succubus: female incubus.

In the "old country", which is Poland in this case, there was an evil spirit called a Zmora. The Zmora would manifest itself in a person by day, and prey on others at night.

As the story goes, a certain young girl had a problem while she was sleeping on her back. She would feel a heaviness on her chest that would choke her if she didn't wake up in time. She went to tell her problem to a wiser woman and the woman told her next time, to pretend she was sleeping and when she felt the heaviness on her chest to grab it and cut it. So the next evening she did as the woman told her, and when the heaviness came on her chest, she grabbed it. The Zmora also had the power to change itself into other objects, so when the girl opened her eyes to see what was on her chest, it was an apple. She then took a knife and cut a piece out of the apple.

The following day, there was a lady in the girl's village with a piece of her cheek missing, and she was branded for life as being a Zmora.

So it is said in an old Polish moral, do not sleep on your back for fear of inviting a Zmora to lie on your chest.

POLISH SUPERSTITIONS

In December, 1973, Allen J. Zales, twenty-three, of North Tonawanda, New York, submitted the following superstitions which he believed to be prevalent among the Polish population of North Tonawanda. Since a number of them have to do with health and ill health, they have been classified under F950, marvelous cures, in the Contents of this publication.

When a baby was sick or cranky, wax drippings from a candle were dripped into a bowl of water and placed under the child's crib. It was left overnight and in the morning it would be examined. The pattern in the bowl made by the wax sticking together was supposed to indicate the source of the reason for the baby's discomfort.

When a child is cutting a tooth, the mother will usually rub whiskey on the sore flesh with her finger.

To the Polish, there is a superstition of death in threes. They say if one person dies, two others of the same status, age, or category will die. When the writer of Perry Mason died, two others from the cast of the Perry Mason television series died. My great uncle recently died. He filled out a group of three from the category of elder family members.

They say that when a dog which is normally quiet has a howling fit, someone in the family will die.

If a person killed a spider, it would surely rain. A ladybug or cricket in the household was a sign of good luck and they would be allowed to roam the house at will.

A man would drink the fresh blood of a newly slaughtered pig to insure his manliness.

When a baby is cranky or colicky, a piece of red cloth is pinned on its chest to deter whatever is troubling the child.

If silverware is accidentally dropped on the floor, it is a sure sign that visitors will call.

If you talk at the dinner table with your mouth full, you will marry an idiot.

Bad weather on a wedding day indicates a good match that will be a successful marriage.

G   OGRES

A DANCE WITH THE DEVIL

The story, called *A Dance with the Devil* by the collector, was told by George Woloszyn, Jr., age nineteen, of North Tonawanda, New York, in November, 1967. Mr. Woloszyn wrote: "I heard the following story when I was about nine years old. The story was told by my grandmother and is supposed to be true. My grandmother was born in Poland and that is where the story takes place."

The motifs in this account are the following: G303.4.5.1, devil detected by his hoofs. While playing cards the devil drops a card on the floor and his partners notice his monstrous feet. G303.10.4.4, devil appears to girl who wants an escort for a dance. G303.17, the devil's disappearance from the world. G303.3.1.17, devil appears as ladies and gentlemen. T330, anchorites under temptation.

The classic myth of Proserpine and Pluto is reflected in the end of the story.

There was a young girl in a small town called Czestochowa. She planned to be a nun. A few days before she was to leave for the convent there was a dance in the town. Persuaded by a few friends she reluctantly went to the dance.

When they arrived she went and sat all alone. A young man, a stranger in the town was able to talk her into dancing with him. After a few dances she felt at ease with the young stranger. After a while he even got her to have a few drinks. Eventually she became drunk and became very intimate with the man. When he saw her holy scapular he laughed at her and told her to take it off. At first she wouldn't but later consented to his request. As they danced someone noticed that the young man had no feet, but instead had hooves. Everyone began to scream and suddenly the devil appeared in his usual appearance. Suddenly the earth below them opened, swallowing the devil and the girl.

The moral of this story is a religious moral. It is told trying to teach the children always to wear their scapular for as long as they wear it the devil can never take them.

A WITCH'S CURSE

The legend, called *A Witch's Curse* by the collector, was written in 1968 by Shirley Placek, then eighteen, of Niagara Falls, New York. Concerning her account, she wrote: "Just recently, my family and I were watching a scary movie which had to do with voodoo and curses. After the movie was over, my grandmother told us that she could write a book on incidents concerning curses and voodoo. She is from Poland and is in her late sixties and she loves to tell us all her stories, most of which concern her life in the Old Country."

The identifying motif in this account is G263.4, witch causes sickness.

This story is of a witch who put curses on anyone she disliked. This didn't bother anyone until the curses started coming true. One incident which my grandmother told me about was that of her girlfriend named Anna. Anna was dating the witch's nephew, John, and although she wasn't serious about him, he was thinking in terms of marriage with her. She had always wanted to leave the little village she lived in and move to the city.

She left for the city against John's will and the witch hated her for hurting her nephew, so she therefore put a spell on Anna. The witch swore that at the time Anna gives birth to her first child, she would die.

Anna never forgot this curse and when she finally did get married, she was petrified of the thought of having a baby, for it surely meant her death. When she finally did get pregnant, all she could think of was her death. She had never told her husband about the curse because she knew that he would laugh at her.

When the time for the baby to be born arrived, she had given up all hope of living. She was delirious before giving birth and she was talking about the curse and her going to die. The nurses immediately got in touch with the witch's nephew and he came down to the hospital to tell Anna that the curses didn't mean anything. Anna was on the brink of death, but something inside her was fighting for life. She had the baby and she lived. The reason for all those other curses coming true was that people thought so much of dying and were so scared of the curse that they actually did die. It was all in their minds. Anna would have died also if it wasn't for that faint spark of life she had in her to live.

The Pot of Milk

The Pot of Milk was written in 1964 by Kathy Golda, eighteen, of Niagara Falls, New York. She stated: "This tale was told to me by my grandmother on February 6, 1964. She was born in the town in which this story was supposed to have taken place and she claims that it is a true story."

The central motif is G269.10, witch punishes person who incurs her ill will. Another motif is E761.5.1, life token; pot breaks.

In the early 1900's in Poland in the small town of Poznan, the people there were very religious but also clung to their superstitions as faithfully as their religion. At this time it was common for gypsies to roam the countryside begging from door to door.

On a small hill overlooking the river lived a family: a mother and her three daughters; the father had died when the children were very young. The mother scarcely made a living for herself and her children.

One morning while the mother was out working in the fields, a lone gypsy woman knocked at the door begging for food. The girls were just warming milk for breakfast. They could not offer her any because this was all they had. The gypsy, angered at this, said they would be sorry. As one of the girls carried the pot of milk to the table, it suddenly set ablaze and fell crashing to the floor. Realizing that the gypsy had put a curse on them, they turned to follow her to beg her forgiveness. She vanished and was nowhere to be found.

The girls returned home very unhappy because they had not only been rude to their visitor but had also lost the last of their food. And upon their return to their home, they found the pot of milk heating on the stove as if nothing had happened.

ANIMAL DUNG

In February, 1967, Marc Bloustein, sixteen, of Tonawanda, New York, wrote for the collector the following account of a witch's curse. He did not give it a title or say anything about its background except that it happened in Poland.

The controlling motif is G269.10, witch punishes person who incurs her ill will.

During the latter part of the nineteenth century, there lived somewhere in Poland a professional witch. It happened one day that a neighbor of this witch insulted her. The witch, being of a very temperamental and irritable nature, immediately placed a curse upon her discourteous neighbor. By this curse, the neighbor, until he made an apology in front of the whole village, would find, every time he turned around, some animal dung beside him. Sure enough, from that time on, every time the neighbor turned around, there lay some animal dung. Finally the poor man was forced to return and apologize to the witch so that the curse might be lifted. When he had done this, amazingly as it had appeared, all of the animal dung disappeared and he was plagued no more.

THE SWAMP

The tale called *The Swamp* by the collector was written in February, 1967, by Linda Ross, seventeen, of Tonawanda, New York. Her informant was Mr. Borowski, about whom she wrote: "He is my study hall teacher. He is from Poland where I think he lived in the rural areas. I think this because as he told me the stories he tried to impress upon me the fact that the country folk believed these stories. The stories were told to him by his grandmother. He also told me that these country folk were very religious, as shown by their references to the devil."

Miss Ross, after writing the following two stories added: "I was told that the reason for the brevity of folk tales was that they were generally told to children."

The central motif of *The Swamp* is G303.6.3, natural phenomena accompanying the devil's appearance.

One story is about a man who had the habit of getting roaring drunk quite regularly. On his way home from these binges he had to pass a large swamp, in the midst of which was a small but deep lake. This man felt pulled toward this lake. One night when he could resist the pull of the swamp and lake no longer, he fell into the lake and drowned. When the story was told, it was said that the devil had taken him because of his evil ways.

THE DEVIL

The Devil, so called by the collector, was also written in February, 1967, by Linda Ross, seventeen, of Tonawanda, New York. (See *The Swamp*, preceding for information on Miss Ross's informant.)

The main motif is G303.5, how the devil is dressed.

The next story takes place on a night similar to our Hallowe'en, the only difference being that adults may take part in this event. This story I was told was often told to children to remind them to lead the 'good life'.

It was after midnight on this Hallowe'en and everyone was in the street with their costumes on. Suddenly there came a priest hurrying to give a dying man his last rites. As was the custom when a priest passed, everyone fell on their knees, making the sign of the cross, and prayed. However, there was one man dressed in the costume of a devil who would not kneel.

When it came time to remove the costumes, this man's would not come off. Since he did not believe in God and would not ask forgiveness, he was forced to live the rest of his life as a devil, shut away from all men.

STRANGE WINDS BLOW *

Another Polish-American legend emanating from the Christian religion is called *Strange Winds Blow* by the informant, Richard Ciesielski of Cheektowaga, New York, who wrote it for me in 1967. It was told to him by his grandmother, Mrs. Mary Naczek, who was born and reared in Buffalo, New York, but whose parents came from Poland.

The devil motifs under G303 are numerous in the Thompson Motif Index of Folk Literature. In this story there are three distinct ones. G303.3.4.4., devil as wind, found in Jewish lore; and G303.3.4.4.1., devil as whirlwind, persons met by him are killed or maimed, found in Wessman's Finnish-Swedish collection, both would be one distinct motif.

G303.15.4., devils haunt tree, would be another motif of interest.

---

* Reprinted from *New York Folklore Quarterly*, Volume III, Number 4 (Dec., 1974) pp. 286 — 294, "Polish-American Church Legends" by Catherine Harris Ainsworth.

Still another motif is G303.16.11., various holy persons save one from devil, as in G303.16.11.4., saint expels devil to hell, and is found in Irish myth and in the French <u>Nouvelles de Sens.</u> The motif is found also under G303.16.11.5., saint's dispute with devil, and is discussed by Loomis in <u>White Magic</u> (p. 76) in which numerous saints have rid persons or places of devils by various magic tricks as well as by dialogue and debate.

In my grandmother's early days she recalls, when on a warm summer day, that when the wind picks up in strength and forms a swirling motion with the leaves, it means that the devil was in the center of the shirling action dancing with the leaves. There was a man in the neighborhood who might be called the black sheep of the flock. This man had a habit of picking the leaves off nearby bushes and chewing on them, as a cowboy on a straw of hay. One day this man had picked and was chewing a leaf from a bush, where just previously there had been this swirling wind action. The man from that instant did not talk or act as himself, but instead would curse and swear at everyone and everything. The people of the neighborhood, suspecting that he might be possessed of the devil, told him to go to a Catholic church and see a person with a clean soul or without more than his hereditary sin. The man was taken to Corpus Christi Church in Buffalo. The priest, who faced with the problem, had asked the devil possessing the man many questions in regard to his presence and attempts with this man. The devil cursed the priest and as the discussion continued, the devil increased in anger until he had left the man to be free of his own actions once again. This story is said to be true and many a person from the surrounding vicinity had come to witness the shocking discussion between the priest and the devil.

H TESTS

BOY OR GIRL

Boy or Girl was written in 1964 by Clifford H. Hanlon, twenty-four, of Williamsville, New York. Miss JoAnn Godamski told him the story in June, 1964, and said that it had been in her family for at least three generations.

The motif, H528, guessing sex of unborn child, is applicable here.

The story is Polish folklore and it gives a test which shows if a woman has had any children, what sex and how many. It will also predict for an unmarried girl how many children she can expect and even what sex they will be.

The necessary equipment for this test consists of an ordinary pencil and a threaded needle. For this test to be successful the following steps must be carefully followed. The needle is stuck in the eraser of the pencil and the thread is securely wrapped around the hand of the person performing the test. It is important that this person be a female from a different family than the girl being tested. Then the tester's elbow is placed on a table and the pencil is suspended so that the point is over the pulse in the wrist of the subject. If the pencil starts to rotate it means that the girl will have a baby. Then if the pencil changes direction such that it swings up and down the arm the baby will be a boy. If on the other hand the pencil swings across the wrist the baby will be a girl. If the pencil then comes to rest it means the girl will only have one child. If it begins to swing in a circle again she will have two children and the sex is determined in the same way. The number of times the pencil goes through this routine will be the number of children the girl will have.

The girl from which I heard this story is firmly convinced of its validity. She swears that it worked with her mother who has nine children, and on her sister who has two. Even the sex of the child came in the order predicted.

J   THE WISE AND THE FOOLISH

THE JOLLY TAILOR

In 1968, William Lukaszonas, eighteen, of Niagara Falls, New York, related *The Jolly Tailor*. About it he wrote: "I heard this tale at home a couple of days ago. My sister told it to me after our Thanksgiving dinner, 1968. She heard it while she was in college. I heard it sometime earlier when I was a boy."

This is tale type 1640. The outstanding motifs are J115.4, clever tailor; L113.9, tailor as hero; and H38.2.1, tailor married to princess betrays trade by calling for needle and thread.

In a little town in Poland, there once lived a handsome tailor named Mr. Nitechka. He was a very happy and pleasant man but he was so thin he could pass through the eye of his own needle. Being so thin, he always ate spaghetti. On holidays he would look most handsome with his beard done up in curls.

One day while sewing in his tailor shop an old lady came to him with a wound. He sewed up the wound which healed beautifully. She was so thankful to Mr. Nitechka that in return she told him his fortune. She told him if he picked any Sunday and kept on traveling west he would come to a city where he would become king. That night, while lying in bed, he thought it over and decided it was impossible but the following Sunday he decided to try it. After walking west for some distance a strong wind developed and Mr. Nitechka, being so thin, was picked up by the wind and carried for miles and miles. He finally landed softly in a wheat field right in the arms of a scarecrow. He started to talk to the scarecrow and after telling him why he was traveling west he finally convinced the scarecrow to come along.

After some time they came upon a revolving house and after it stopped revolving they decided to enter. Inside they viewed a nobleman and his family sitting on a fire and eating hot coals. The nobleman requested that Mr. Nitechka entertain his family so he sang a song about the Blessed Virgin Mary. When they heard the song they started to scream and throw fits. Mr. Nitechka finally realized they were evil spirits. The devil then told him that in a nearby city the king had just died and that if he would marry his daughter he would become king. Having refused, Mr. Nitechka and the scarecrow were taken prisoners. Soon after, they escaped and continued west toward the nearby city. As they neared the city, the people surrounded them saying that ever since the king's death it's been raining. If it didn't stop soon the city would be destroyed by a flood. It only rained on their city and the weather was beautiful on the outskirts. The king's daughter, who hadn't stopped crying since his death, promised to marry whoever would save the city. Mr. Nitechka and the scarecrow spent the next three days trying to solve the problem. Finally Mr. Nitechka figured that the king was such a great and holy man that when he died and went to heaven he made a hole as big as the city in the sky. Mr. Nitechka got his needle and miles and miles of thread. All the people from the city brought their ladders. Mr. Nitechka and the scarecrow attached all the ladders and leaned them against the sky. The handsome tailor climbed up the ladder and started to sew the hole in the sky with his needle and thread. After a few days of sewing the rain finally stopped. The people rejoiced and the princess dried her tears.

Mr. Nitechka, being the new king, married the lovely princess and they lived happily ever after.

THE LOST HAM

The Lost Ham was told in 1974 by James Szumla, eighteen, of Buffalo, New York. He heard it from "an old classmate from grade school and high school." The central action of the anecdote should be classified between J1650 and J1699, miscellaneous clever acts, of The <u>Motif Index of Folk Literature.</u>

The people of Poland are very religious and very fearful of God, which causes them to be good. But this one man was not good all the time. So this one priest decided to do something about it. He had a little talk with this man and told him that if he does not do right all the time something bad will happen to him.

One day this man was walking down a country road and found a ham lying on the roadside that led into a town. So the teaching of doing the right got the best of him and he walked through the streets yelling loudly, "**Who lost a** (then in a whisper) . . . ham? **Who lost a** . . . ham?"

Because no one knew what he was yelling about, he took the ham home and had it for supper.

THE MEAN RICH MAN

The Mean Rich Man was written in 1977 by Lois M. Cox, twenty three, of Niagara Falls, New York. She stated that she heard it "over the Easter vacation sitting in my sister's house". Her informant was Victor Taylor, her future brother-in-law, who heard it from his grandmother, who came from Poland.

The motifs present in the tale are J1210, clever man puts another out of countenance; and L143, poor man surpasses rich.

Once there was a rich man. He was very mean and he was always thinking about how to fool the men who worked for him and to get them to work too hard for very little money. So one day he goes into town and he sees this simple man standing in the street, not doing anything, just standing with his mouth open. He went up to him and said, "Do you want some work?"

And the simple man said, "Sure."

And the rich man laughed to himself and thought, "I will now get this simple man to work very hard and pay him very little."

So they went to the rich man's house. By then it was too late to work so they went to bed and in the morning the rich man woke up the simple man and told him it was time to go out in the field and go to work. So the simple man got up and ate a good breakfast and started to leave for the field. The rich man said, "You have too far to go to work to come home for lunch."

So the simple man said, "You give me my lunch now so that no one has to bring me my lunch way out there."

The rich man was all too glad to give him his lunch now so that no one had to stop work just to take him his food. When the simple man finished his lunch, he got up to go out into the fields and the rich man said, "Why don't you eat your supper now so that you don't have to come home early?" The rich man thought, "He can't eat much now and my wife won't have to feed him later."

So the simple man said, "All right." And he ate his supper.

Then the rich man said, "Now go out into the field and go to work."

And the simple man said, "Oh, no. All my life I've had the same habit. I always go right to sleep after supper and I'm not going to change now."

And so the simple man went to sleep. The rich man now felt like a fool.

K   DECEPTIONS

HOW KRAKOW WAS NAMED

How Krakow Was Named was written in 1972 by Judy Gilbert, eighteen, of North Tonawanda, New York. Her grandmother, who was born near the city in which the story took place, told her the story "over the Thanksgiving holiday" of 1972.

The motifs from K800 to K999 deal with killing or maiming by deception. K839.3 is the motif, victim enticed into drinking by oversalting his food.

There once was a man named Krakus who lived in the country which is now called Poland. Now this man lived in a tiny farming hamlet where the people owned their own animals and lived independently. In this hamlet there was a huge boulder which covered up the entrance to a dark cave which was the home of a man-eating dragon. This dragon constantly terrorized the people and ate the cows, sheep and other farm animals of them. Krakus was a brave man who wanted to be recognized as a hero so one day he decided to kill the dragon and save the people of the hamlet from further harm. Krakus had a plan, he captured a ram, killed it, and cleaned its insides compeltely. After he did this he stuffed the ram with a mixture of sulfa, straw, and hot tar. He then went to the cave and threw the ram to the dragon for dinner. Because the dragon was hungry he quickly swallowed the whole ram without even stopping to chew it. Soon the mixture inside the stuffed ram began to burn and the dragon's stomach began to burn and feel very uncomfortable. The dragon could no longer stand the pain so he dragged himself to a nearby river, which was called the Wistua, to take a cool drink to soothe his stomach. He drank and drank the river water but the pain persisted; soon the dragon was filled with so much water that he couldn't move one inch. Krakus saw that his plan had worked; he jumped on the huge dragon and cut off his head with his sword. The people of the hamlet declared Krakus their hero and the king of their country; they also named their city Krakow, after the brave man who killed the man-eating dragon.

WAWEL TALE

Wawel Tale was written in 1973 by Kerry Krzystek, eighteen, of Niagara Falls, New York. This is another version of the tale of how Krakow was named and the same motif numbers apply; K800–K999, killing or maiming by deception; and K839.3, victim enticed into drinking by oversalting his food.

This summer my sister and I went to visit Poland. When we were in Krakow my Aunt Mary, who lived in Poland all her life, was our guide. She took us to all the historical places. On our second day while in Krakow she took us to Wawel Castle built on a hill and facing a river. While we were waiting for our English interpreter, because our Polish wasn't very good, we took a walk down the hill. Walking around we came across a cave under the castle. Since my aunt teaches history, she told us the story about the cave.

It seems during the Medieval Age a dragon lived in that cave and every Monday a pretty young maiden had to be his supper. A young princess was picked as his next meal, but a young shoemaker was in love with her and tried to think of a scheme to save her. Thinking and thinking, he finally killed a lamb and stuffed it with inflammable materials.

On this specific Monday he threw the lamb to the dragon, which he ate. Later, the dragon became hot and ran to the river. He kept on drinking and drinking 'til he finally exploded. Now in front of his cave a monument of him, the dragon, is built in his honor. Every night fire is supposed to come out of his mouth, but it seems it never works.

THE RED TOMATO

The Red Tomato was written in 1977 by Danielle Osypiewski, twenty-six, of North Tonawanda, New York. This experience was related by her husband's grandmother, who also bore the name Osypiewski. Danielle stated: "I couldn't get a real folktale that had been handed down, so I used a story that had happened to Babci herself instead. It also involved my landlady, Mrs. Krawczyk, who is now 94.

A motif applicable to this anecdote is K1840, deception by substitution.

Both Babci and Mrs. Krawczyk were avid gardeners. They still do some gardening. And while Babci was content to let things grow in their own good time, Mrs. Krawczyk had to be the first on the block to have something ripe. Her favorite was tomatoes. It still is. And she would travel around the neighborhood checking out everyone else's progress. She would make a special point of letting everyone know and see her first ripening tomatoes. She was a frequent sight, especially at Babci's in the summer, each time asking, "You got any ripe tomatoes yet?"

She got definite satisfaction from knowing that she was always the first one.

Finally Babci decided, "I'll fix her." She sent her daughter to the store to buy a small red tomato. A big one would have been too obvious. When the daughter returned with it, Babci tied it onto one of the vines near the back, but so that you could see it. Then she started to water her garden.

When Mrs. Krawczyk came along and asked the usual question, Babci said, "Yes, see, it's right over there." Mrs. Krawczyk wanted to go look at it, but Babci said, "No, you can't walk in the garden when it's wet."

Mrs. Krawczyk never asked again about Babci's tomatoes.

A WISE OLD WOMAN

A Wise Old Woman was written in 1976 by K. Hogg, twenty, of Amherst, New York. She heard the tale from her mother's husband, Joseph Gladysz, who heard it from his grandfather from Poland.

The central motif is K2365.1, enemy induced to give up siege by pretending to have plenty of food. This motif is found in German and Japanese collections and in the classical authors, Herodotus and Ovid.

Once, a very long time ago, a little town outside Poland was being captured. The enemy was waiting outside the gate until the town died of hunger or surrendered, which ever came first. In the town, people had already died of hunger and sickness. The ruler of the town spoke to the remaining people and told them that they must surrender before they all died of hunger.

An old woman stepped up to him and said, "If you do as I say the town will be saved."

With no other choice they did as she said. "First bring me a cow," she requested. The people searched the town and found a cow that an old man had hidden. Then they brought the cow to her. "Next," she said, "bring me a bushel of meal."

The townspeople scraped up barely a bushel and returned to the old woman. She watered the meal and fed it to the cow. When night fell she ordered the men to open the gate and release the cow. The enemy grabbed the cow and brought it to their leader.

The leader figured they let the cow out to graze. Knowing that they themselves were starving, he ordered the cow killed for dinner. In opening the cow, they saw the meal. Seeing this, the leader said, "If they have enough meal to feed their animals, we will have to wait here too long for them to surrender. We will starve." So they packed up and left that very night. The townspeople with joy gave praise to the old woman and made her comfortable for the rest of her life.

M   ORDAINING THE FUTURE

THE FALLEN PICTURE

In 1964, Ronald Danielewiz, twenty, of Niagara Falls, New York, wrote the following legend called *The Fallen Picture* by the collector. He stated that he heard it a year earlier at his home from his grandmother.

The main motif is M341, death prophesied.

On a cold autumn morning last year while I was attending Sunday mass, little did I know that I would come in contact with a legend. Above the altar at my church there is a large picture. During the mass this Sunday the picture fell with a thunderous roar. The people became frightened. An uneasy feeling remained for the remainder of the mass, even with the priest. While leaving the church after mass, I noticed many of the older people discussing the incident in a sincere and somewhat eerie manner. When I reached home I was quite concerned about what had happened and questioned my grandmother.

After hearing about the incident, I noticed a look of worry upon her face. I asked her to explain this. It seems that during her childhood in Poland there was a belief, legend, that if a picture fell during mass someone had died. I then became interested in finding out if this were true. A few days later I was informed that someone had died at the approximate time that the picture fell. I wondered, is this a coincidence or is it the legend being true. I'll never know.

THE VIOLIN

David Nosal, nineteen, of Buffalo, New York, wrote *The Violin* in 1964. About it he wrote: "I heard this story when I was about 8 years old. It was told to me by my grandfather in his home here in Buffalo. My grandfather came from Poland."

The main motif is a familiar one, M211, man sells soul to devil. Another motif would come between K100 and K299, deceptive bargains.

There once was a young man who could play the violin very well. He loved to play the violin and was afraid of growing old. He wanted to retain his youth so that he could keep playing. One day the young man made a deal with the devil. The devil promised the young man youth forever if he would give the devil his soul when he dies. The young man asked the devil how he would die if he was to be a young man forever. The devil said that the only condition was if the young man ever stepped in Rome he would die. The young man figured he would never go to Rome so he traded his soul for youth. But as time went by the young man would drink. One day he went into a bar and died. The name of the bar was Rome. From that time on the young man's violin hangs in a room and at a certain time every day it begins to play.

N   CHANCE AND FATE

THE JACKRABBIT

The Jackrabbit was written in 1969 by Michael A. Janda, eighteen, of North Tonawanda, New York. The background of the legend was interwoven in the telling of it.

It should be considered a modified and tempered version of the usual cemetery legend. Motif N384.2 is related to the main motif of falling into the grave as revealed in this legend. N384.2 is death in graveyard; person's clothing is caught; the person thinks something awful is holding him; he dies of fright.

This story I am about to tell was told to me by my grandfather, Mr. Joseph Rzepa, about three years ago at Christmas time.

This incident happened when he was about twelve or thirteen years old, about the year 1909 or 1910, in a town called Czarna (Black Forest) in Poland. He was late coming home, was somewhere where he couldn't remember, and he wanted to take a short cut through a cemetery located in back of his house. On approaching the cemetery, he saw that the rear wooden fence of the cemetery was down. This saved him the trouble of climbing over it. Since it was evening and since there was no lights in those days, he had a hard time seeing where he was going. About half way through the cemetery he fell into a freshly dug grave. As he was trying to figure out how to get out of the eight feet deep hole, he felt something moving around his feet. He said he was scared silly. Since it was dark, he couldn't see what it was. He finally found a shovel in the grave, spiked in on the side wall of the grave, and boosted himself out. When he got home he didn't tell his mother what had happened, but he couldn't sleep all that night. The next day he was still wondering what could have been in that grave. His mother sent him up the road to a neighbor's house to borrow a cup of salt. It just so happened that he was the keeper of the grounds at the cemetery. He told my grandfather that he found a 15 pound jackrabbit in a grave he dug yesterday. The jackrabbit was drowned because it had rained during the night, so the keeper was going to have it for dinner. When my grandfather heard that, he breathed a sigh of relief. What could have been a body was just a jackrabbit.

THE KNIFE IN THE GRAVE

Daniel William Swiatek, eighteen, of Buffalo, New York, wrote *The Knife in the Grave* in 1964. He stated that the story had been told to him by his mother quite a while ago. His mother had acquired the story from her grandmother who had lived in Poland.

The main motif in this tale is N384.2, death in graveyard; person's clothing is caught; the person thinks something awful is holding him and dies of fright.

In a Polish village near the Russian border there was a man who was very unpopular with the people. Being the biggest coward of them all he did the most boasting. A fellow townsman made a bet with him that he would be afraid to go into the cemetery at night and stick a dagger in a grave near the middle of the cemetery. Due to the amount wagered the coward went out to the cemetery at night and never returned. When the villagers went there, they found him dead from fright. He had apparently stuck the knife in his coat and tried to run away. The coat was stuck fast and he died from fear of something holding him.

P   SOCIETY

CHRISTMAS DINNER

The following Christmas custom was written by James Orzechowski, seventeen of Niagara Falls, New York. It was told to him by his father, Edward Orzechowski.

See the motifs under P600——P699 for customs and P634 for feasts.

On Christmas Day, 1965, after our annual Christmas dinner, I asked my father how he used to celebrate the Christmas meal when he was a young boy. This is what he told me. On the day before Christmas, his family would have two very small and light meals during the day, which would be to them a sort of fast. That night, before the large dinner, he and his family would pass around a piece of wafer, called oplatek in Polish. One person would hold the wafer and wish happiness, a good life and good health to the other person while he (other person) broke the wafer. Then all would say a prayer and eat the wafer. This symbolized receiving God in their hearts. For the dinner, the people had fish, usually herring, a cabbage soup, called kapusta, with beans and vegetables, and a kind of porridge with prunes with a potato soup called boszch. A great deal of this custom still holds in most Polish homes today.

T SEX

FINDING A SPOUSE

Finding A Spouse was written in 1964 by William F. Seiler, twenty-three, of Williamsville, New York. His informant was a Polish-American friend, Mr. L. Wrona.

The applicable motif in this bit of custom lore is T3, omens in love affairs.

A method of finding the direction from which one's spouse will come, has been handed down through the generations by many Polish-American sects.

On Christmas eve, after a festive meal has been enjoyed by the entire family, the unwed members assemble on the porch to await the appearance of the first star. After this star has been sighted, the oldest unmarried child steps forward, and calls out into the night. The direction in which the cold winter air carries these sounds is believed to be the direction from which one's spouse will come. This ritual is repeated by all the unwed children, each taking his respective turn.

POLISH MARRIAGE CUSTOMS

The following Polish marriage customs were submitted in 1971 by Mary Therrien, eighteen, of North Tonawanda, New York. She heard them from her aunt, Mrs. Natalie Bernhardt, of Williamsville, New York, who heard them from her mother when she was a little girl. Mrs. Bernhardt is from a Polish family. Her grandfather was an immigrant from Poland to the coal mines in Nanticoke, Pennsylvania, where her father worked also.

T130, marriage customs, is the obvious motif for this account.

In the old country, Poland, most of the people in our family were small subsistence farmers. The biggest thing in their lives was a marriage. The only gifts that these poor people could give the bride and groom were the vegetables and fruits from their farm. Everyone wished the couple well and, since they could not afford the material benefits to give the newly-weds, they well-wished them by singing. The song wished them a happy and prosperous life together.

Today, although most of my relatives are able to give more than vegetables, and none of my relatives are farmers, they still sing this song to the couple.

More importantly, the relatives of the bride and groom give the groom a hat made of vegetables and fruits. These are supposed to wish the couple well in bearing children. All the men in the wedding party dance with the wife to show her she must have endurance and strength to live a married life. Finally, the couple dances alone, to show they are totally independent and must be successful on their own. Then there is usually three days of dancing and drinking to celebrate the happy occasion.

A POLISH WEDDING

The following booklet from a Polish wedding in November, 1972, was submitted in the same month by Susan Janik, eighteen, of Niagara Falls, New York. The wedding probably took place in the Niagara Falls area. The booklet demonstrates well the transition and blending of old and new world customs, songs, and languages.

This item has been classified under T130, marriage customs.

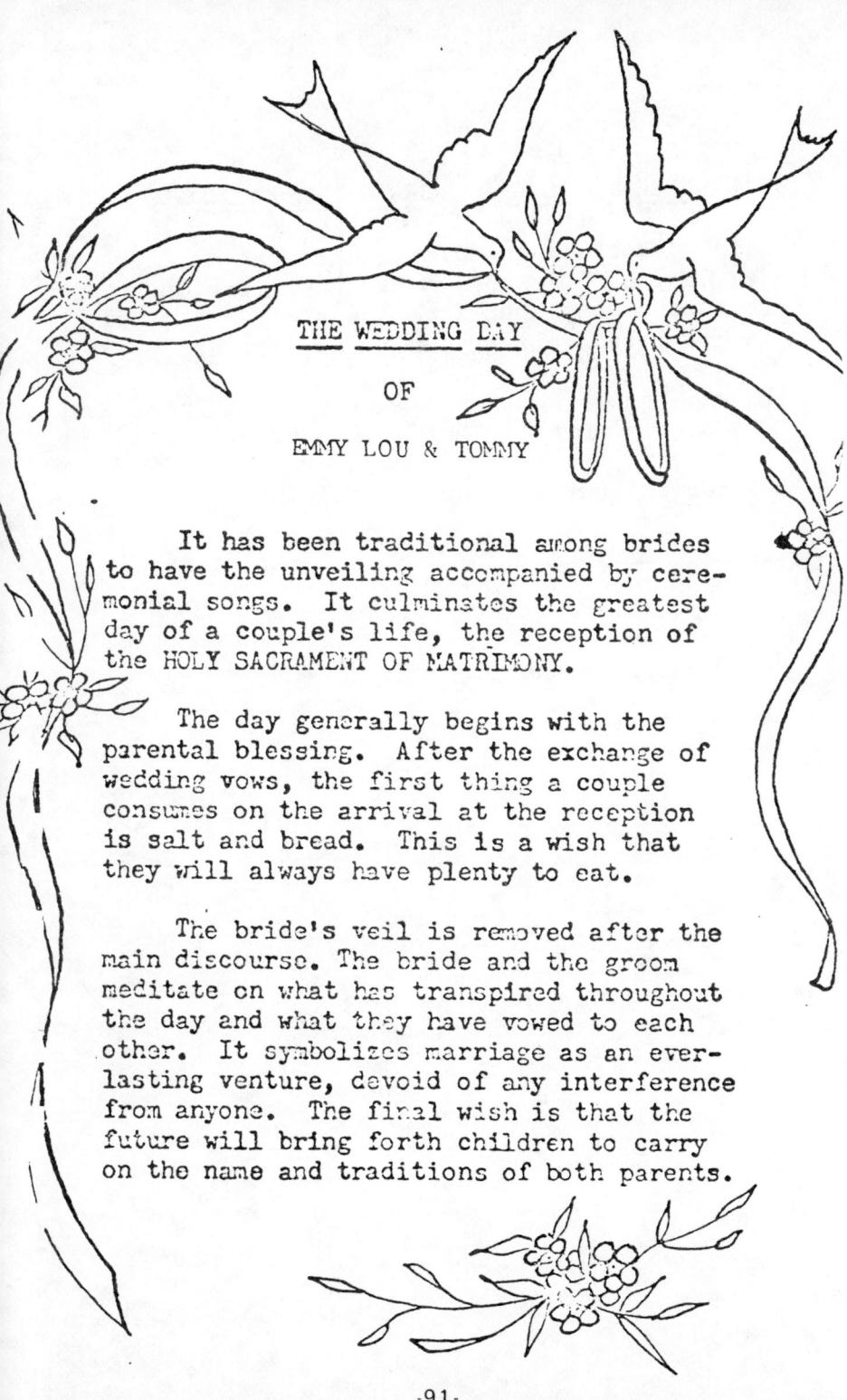

THE WEDDING DAY

OF

EMMY LOU & TOMMY

It has been traditional among brides to have the unveiling accompanied by ceremonial songs. It culminates the greatest day of a couple's life, the reception of the HOLY SACRAMENT OF MATRIMONY.

The day generally begins with the parental blessing. After the exchange of wedding vows, the first thing a couple consumes on the arrival at the reception is salt and bread. This is a wish that they will always have plenty to eat.

The bride's veil is removed after the main discourse. The bride and the groom meditate on what has transpired throughout the day and what they have vowed to each other. It symbolizes marriage as an everlasting venture, devoid of any interference from anyone. The final wish is that the future will bring forth children to carry on the name and traditions of both parents.

BELOVED MOTHER (SERDECZNA MATKO)

Beloved Mother, guardian of the nation,
Hearken, oh hearken, to our supplication.
//Your loyal children from the plain and city,
We kneel beseeching your great love and pity.//

To whom shall we turn to, we poor souls of Eve,
Pleadingly we call Mother how we grieve,
//Your heart's a refuge opened ever wide,
Mother protect us, keep us at your side.//

AS LOVELY GREEN GRASS GROWS (ROSNIE TRAWKA)

1. As lovely green grass grows,
   Throughout this promised land,
   Before the main altar,
   You've give Tommy your hand.
2. You've given Tommy your hand,
   He gave a golden band.
   Your eyes swelled up with tears,
   Before your friends on hand.
3. Twelve lovely white petals
   Attached to this white rose,
   Twelve heavenly angels
   Serve the bride they chose.
4. The first angel has brought
   A candle's brilliance;
   The second angel brought
   A lily's full fragrance.
5. The third angel has brought
   A lovely bouquet to hold;
   The fourth angel has brought
   Your wedding band of gold.
6. The fifth angel has come with
   Blessings from the Lord;
   The sixth angel has come
   With matrimonial accord.

7. The remaining six angels
   Come with a crown so keen,
   They'll place it on your head
   As if upon a queen.
8. You promised to be true,
   Love, honor, and obey;
   In all your days ahead
   Uphold the vows made today.
9. Remember to be good
   And live in wedded bliss,
   And in our presence now
   Honor him with a kiss.
10. Remember, Marylou, be true,
    Your right hand on the cross,
    You've pledged your life and love,
    To Tommy who is the "Boss".
11. Oh, wedding gown and crown,
    Somehow you make me sad,
    You make me feel that
    I'm losing my Mom and Dad.
12. And yet with Mom and Dad
    No longer shall you live,
    But only with your Tommy
    To whom your life you give.
13. Remember to be good
    And live a life of prayer,
    And in a year or two
    Present him with an heir.

OH, MY LEANDER WREATH (ACH MOJ WIANKU)

1. Ach, moj wianku Lewandowy, Nie spadaj,
   Nie spadaj mi z glowy.
2. Bo jak ci mi wianek spadnie, zaraz moje,
   Zaraz moje liczko zbladnie.
3. Wsadzili mnie do komory i zdejmuja,
   I zdejmuja wianek z glowy.
4. I wlozyli to czapczysko, kaza kochac
   I szanowac to mezysko
5. A ja meza zlapie za szyje, trzeba kochac
   I szanowac poki zyje.

SHE FELL FROM A CHERRY TREE (SPADLA Z WISNI)

Spadla z wisni, widzielismy
I podarla fartuszek, szywalismy
Jeden trzymal, drugi zszywal
A ten trzeci co doleci, porozrywal
Nie rozrywaj, nie rob szkody
Choc ze do mnie do lozeczka
Dam ci miody.

THE GROOM

A Pan Mlody, nie od tego
Zafunduje nam jednego
Wiec Panowie jego zdrowie
Niechaj zyje nam.
Wiec Panowie jego zdrowie
Niechaj zyje nam.
Wiec Panowie jego zdrowie
Niechaj zyje nam.

LET ME CALL YOU SWEETHEART

Let me call you Sweetheart,
    I'm in love with you.
Let me hear you whisper,
    That you love me true,
Keep the lovelight glowing,
    In your eyes so true.
Let me call you Sweetheart,
    I'm in love with You.

V RELIGION

THE WHITE LILY

The White Lily was written in 1964 by Roger T. Czarnecki of West Seneca, New York, who explains the background in the legend itself, which follows.

The central motif is V225.1, devotee of Virgin not buried in consecrated ground has lily issue from mouth so that his grave is made known. The same legend is found in both Spanish and Italian folklore.

I heard a folk story about four years ago from my grandmother. She is of Polish descent and spent the first twenty years of her life living in a small village outside Warsaw, Poland. The story took place about sixty years ago. It is a story about my grandmother's sister Katty, and Katty's young daughter, Lillian.

In the spring of 1902, my great-aunt Katty gave birth to a beautiful baby girl. She named the baby Lillian because she had milk white skin and platinum blond hair. The baby hardly ever cried. As soon as Lillian was old enough to help, she helped her mother with the family and helped her father with the farm chores all day long. When anyone in the family became sick, Lillian spent endless hours caring for the sick person and nursing them back to good health. At this time she was no more than eight or nine years of age. Even in the bitter cold of winter, she would go outside barefooted, walk to the barn, and care for the animals. She walked about a quarter of a mile each day to obtain water from a stream for her mother, still in her bare feet. In the winter of 1911, a smallpox epidemic hit the area. Almost all of the children were very sick and in danger of death. Lillian, on the other hand, was in perfect health. She spent all of her time caring for her sick brothers and sisters. Of the five children stricken with the disease, four died; only the oldest boy survived. He got well largely through the incessant care given to him by his little sister. She acted like an angel of mercy, always thinking of others, but never of herself.

A year later, again in the dead of winter, Lillian caught a severe cold. This was undoubtedly caused by her walking around outside in her bare feet. In a matter of two days, she was dead. My grandmother told me that Lillian looked like an angel in her casket; she was dressed in pure white. There seemed to be a luminescent glow around her body as she laid in the casket. She was buried in the small village cemetery on a bitterly cold winter day. About three weeks later, after a mild snowfall, my grandmother and her sister Katty decided to go to the gravesite. To their astonishment, there was a fresh, snow white lily growing up through the snow on the spot where the angelic child, Lillian, was buried. My grandmother said that she would not have believed it, but she saw it with her own two eyes! This is a true story.

Z   MISCELLANEOUS GROUPS OF MOTIFS

MEET YOU ON FRIDAY

Meet You On Friday was submitted in April, 1976, by Mary Moley, eighteen, of Newfane, New York. According to Miss Moley, the story was told by her mother about her great grandmother, or her mother's grandmother.

The motifs are Z111, death personified; and Z111,5, death (fate) assumes various forms to destroy men.

My great grandmother was from Poland, somewhere near the German border. Granddaughter of the east king of Poland, she married a man of nobility, only because it was arranged. My grandfather owned land, some being in America.

He traveled to America, coming back to her three times, only to father children. The fourth time he came to America she had him traced and decided to follow him. She sold every thing she could, gave things away, packed everything, got the seven children together, and came to America. She followed him to Brooklyn because she was told he was there. She finally caught up with him in Buffalo where he had had an accident and he finally decided to settle down with his family.

When the children had grown, they lived with one of them, not as man and wife.

Her only recreation was to walk to a theatre in Buffalo called the Orpheum Theatre to see a movie and play bingo. One Friday night while walking home from the theatre, a man appeared and began talking with her. She didn't feel a bit ill at ease with him. He walked her home and into the hallway and said, "I'll meet with you on Friday." He didn't say how, when, or why, just that he would see her. She walked in the door happy and excited, unlike herself. She had never thought about dating because she was married.

The grandchildren spoke of the happening all week and were curious of what Friday would bring. My great grandmother didn't say much about it. Religious as she was, she believed she saw the sacred heart.

Friday came, only she never saw it. She had died in her sleep. Her family knew in their hearts that she had met him.

AN ETERNAL JEW

An Eternal Jew was written in 1964 by Kay Micherewicz of Williamsville, New York, when she was a student at the University of Buffalo. She heard it from her father, who in turn heard it from his father. According to Miss Micherewicz, the expression "eternal Jew" is often heard among the Polish people and refers to very, very old people. She believes that the tale reflects the cleverness of the Jewish people and has a counterpart among the Germans.

The central motifs are Z111, death personified; and Z111.2, death magically bound to tree.

When the Lord, Jesus Christ, was still residing among the people in Judea, he wanted to convince himself of how the strangers and homeless were being treated, so he disguised himself as a beggar and started out on his journey. He wandered through many cities and towns and begged for food and shelter for the night. The people, however, looked unfavorably upon vagrants and intruders and quickly turned them away from their doors. And so the Lord went on but as the night drew near and his feet became more tired, he decided to give it one more try and stop at a poorly-looking house. As he knocked at the door, an old man opened it and asked the stranger in. He was made comfortable and invited to share the old man's supper. After they had eaten, the old man brought out some apples which he himself had picked off his apple tree in his garden. They delighted in this delicacy, after which the stranger commented that they were by far the best apples he had tasted. After moments of conversation they both retired for the night.

The next day, the visitor, upon departure, said to his host, "You have been most kind to me and I am very grateful for your hospitality. Therefore, in return for all your favors, I would like to present you with a token of appreciation. You may make a wish of any kind and I will make it come true."

"Stranger," replied the old man, "I am quite happy and content with what I have but there is one thing that annoys me very much. I don't like to have people climb my apple tree and pick my apples. If there is any way I could stop them from doing it, I would be most grateful."

The stranger immediately replied, "I shall cast a magic spell on your apple tree, and if anyone climbs it and picks your apples, he will not be able to come down unless you order him to do so and he returns the apples."

The old man was overwhelmed and thanked the stranger for this favor.

Shortly after the stranger had left, the old man was visited by the Death. She entered without knocking, since she had the power of entering closed doors, and ordered the old man to get ready for his final journey. But the old man was in no hurry to go with the Death. He quickly thought of his magic apple tree and out of curiosity of how the magic would affect the Death, he said, "Since I did not have anything to eat as yet and I can no longer climb my apple tree to pick some apples for my lunch, perhaps you would be kind enough and get me a couple of apples."

The Death agreed and climbed the apple tree. As soon as she picked an apple, she was unable to come down. Screaming and complaining that she had a job to do, that there is a great number of souls she has to deliver before the gates of heaven, and the old man better tell her how to come down. But the old man was in no hurry to die and he replied, "You just stay there where you are, for nobody is in a hurry to go along with you. I, in particular, like to linger on earth for a little while longer."

So the Death, bewitched on the apple tree, enabled the Jew to live on to eternity.